MW01156418

Exciting Books From
WEBB RESEARCH GROUP, PUBLISHERS
→Availability and prices subject to change. This is a *partial* list←

Shipwrecks and Rescues on the Northwest Coast. Bert and Margie Webber.
Amazing true episodes of disasters. $14.95.

Oregon's Seacoast Lighthouses (Includes nearby Shipwrecks). James A.
Gibbs with Bert Webber. Every Oregon coast lighthouse! $14.95.

Oregon's Salty Coast From Explorers to the Present Time, James A. Gibbs
with Bert Webber. Oregon Coast State Park Directory. $12.95.

Terrible Tilly (Tillamook Rock Lighthouse);The Biography of a Lighthouse.
(Near Cannon Beach) (Expanded Edition)Bert and Margie Webber. $12.95.

Yaquina Lighthouses on the Oregon Coast. Dorothy Wall with Bert Webber.
Both Yaquina Bay and Yaquina Head Lighthouses. $10.95.

*Battery Point Light[house] and the Tidal Wave of 1964; Includes St. George
Reef Light[house].* Bert and Margie Webber. (Crescent City, Calif.) $ 9.95.

Bayocean: The Oregon Town That Fell Into the Sea. Bert and Margie
Webber. Includes Salishan, other erosion damages areas. $14.95.

Lakeport: Ghost Town of the South Oregon Coast. Bert and Margie Webber.
Weird shipwreck; grim WW-II Coast Guard duty. $12.95.

I'd Rather Be Beachcombing. Bert and Margie Webber. Emphasizes glass
Japanese fishing floats – when/where/how to find them. $12.95.

Battleship Oregon: Bulldog of the Navy. Bert Webber. The most amazing
battleship ever! Spanish-American, First World War, WW-II $12.95.

Panic! At Fort Stevens Japanese Shell Ft. Stevens, Ore. in WW-II. Bert
Webber. *Documentary* - 146 pictures and maps. $ 9.95.

*Silent Siege-III: Japanese Attacks on North America in World War II; Ships
Sunk, Air raids, Bombs Dropped, Civilians Killed.* Bert Webber. Hundreds
of Japanese attacks on 28 U.S. states – kids killed – and Canada never
reported in papers due to agreement between gov't and press not to cause
public panic. 304 pages, 462 photos, maps. BIG BOOK ! 8½x11 $29.95.

This Is Logging & Sawmilling - Documentary Bert and Margie Webber.
Helicopter logging, Railroad logging, Logging in snow, Fighting forest
fires. 247 unusual photos, maps, 160 pages. BIG BOOK! 8½x11 $19.95.

*The Awesome Caverns of Marble in the Oregon Caves National Monument
Documentary.* Bert & Margie Webber. 240p. Astounding pictures! $14.95.

Oregon Covered Bridges – Expanded Edition [1999]; Bert and Margie Webber.
(6 More Bridges!) Photos, how to visit all standing bridges. $12.95.

"OUR BOOKS ARE HISTORICALLY ACCURATE AND FUN TO READ"

Shipping: Add $2.50 – except big *Silent Siege III, Gold Mining, Logging, Siskiyou Line* $5.95, first book 75¢ each extra book shipped
Books Are Available Through All Book Sellers or Order from Publisher.
Send stamped, self-addressed envelope to speed copy of latest catalog to you.
Visit our color catalog on the Internet   www.pnorthwestbooks.com

WEBB RESEARCH GROUP PUBLISHERS
P.O. Box 314   Medford, OR 97501 USA

Bayocean

One of only five buildings moved off Bayocean Peninsula. Picture, made by Howard Sherwood, shows "pagoda" house being pulled across Rockcrusher Gap at low tide. House was eventually mounted on a foundation in the Cape Mears community.

Bayocean
THE OREGON TOWN THAT FELL INTO THE SEA
[DOCUMENTARY]

INCLUDES ADDITIONAL ERODED AREAS
ALONG THE NORTHWEST COAST

BERT & MARGIE WEBBER

WEBB RESEARCH GROUP

Copyright © 1989 Bert & Margie Webber
All Rights Reserved Under
Berne International Copyright Convention
Under Which Terms No Copies Of This
Material May Be Made By Any Means Whatsoever
Printed in Oregon, U.S.A.

Published May 1989
Second printing July 1992
Third printing March 1996
Fourth Printing March 1999

– NOMINATED –
Creative Non-Fiction Award
OREGON INSTITUTE OF
LITERARY ARTS
–1990–

Published by:
WEBB RESEARCH GROUP PUBLISHERS
Books About the Oregon Country
P. O. Box 314
Medford, OR 97501

The Oregon Coast In Wintertime Is One Of The Most Inhospitable Coasts In The World —U. S. Coast Guard

Library of Congress Cataloging-in-Publication Data

Webber, Bert
　　Bayocean : the Oregon town that fell into the sea : Includes
additional eroded areas along the North West coast : documentary.
　　Includes bibliographical references and index.
　　p.　cm.
　　1. Coast changes – Oregon – Bayocean. 2. Bayocean (Or.) –
History. 3. Coast changes – Oregon. I. Webber, Margie. II.. Title.
　　ISBN 0-936738-40-5 (hard)
　　ISBN 0-936738-37-5 (pbk)
　　GB458.8W38　1989
　　333.91'7137'09794–dc20　　　　　　　　　　　　89-9067
　　　　　　　　　　　　　　　　　　　　　　　　　　CIP

TABLE OF CONTENTS

DEDICATION
TO

FRANCIS DRAKE MITCHELL
1870 — 1965

He bought the first tracts of land at Bayocean in 1907, then worked and lived there nearly half a century. For decades he was the most positive spokesman Bayocean ever had. He saw his dream vanish because of chicanery, then the very land he stood on disintegrated by the ever onrushing, sand-grabbing ocean. During his last years he looked like a bewildered child who had been punished for some infraction he did not understand. Abandoned and alone, he spent his last days at the State Hospital. He is buried in Tillamook Oddfellows Cemetery.

PREFACE

We can imagine the excitement in the eyes and in the mind of Thomas Benton Potter when, in 1906, his son came back from a short vacation and in glowing terms described his visit to Tillamook Spit. Thomas Irving Potter, professionally known as T. Irving Potter, was associated with his father in real estate sales and tract development. It occurs that T. Irving was boating in Tillamook Bay. He spotted a goose as the small boat neared the peninsula so he shot the goose with a revolver. The owner of the rented boat wanted to retrieve the goose so the two men landed on the spit to get it. According to an article in *The Spectator*, a Portland newspaper, "The view from the spot where the goose fell determined the development of Bayocean."

The elder Potter decided the spit would be ideal for a grand vacation resort. Immediately on investigation, T. B. Potter determined to build what he would promote as "the Atlantic City of the West." Potter acquired the land and set out to build his town. He decided to name it "Bayocean," as the ocean was on one side and the bay was on the other. Between the two was a long slender spit of sand, with a mighty dune 140 feet high near the middle, and a knob of trees on the end—Kincheloe Point. Potter would build his town and he would sell building tracts to many hundreds of people. Potter, and a few others, would make money—lots of it. And some people would lose money—lots of it, mostly because, though T. B. Potter and T. Irving Potter (who would do most of the developing), never dreamed their town would eventually fall into the sea one house at a time, including their three-story hotel, over a period of twenty years or so. Cause: Man-created coastal erosion.

In 1952, during a tremendous early-winter storm, the spit was breached in several places. Within days the breaks spread and became a mile wide, allowing the sea water to flow directly into the bay even at low tide. The narrow southern end of the spit was gone, so the northern end became an island. After the usual political haggling, which included a lot of speeches, studies, more studies, and finally funding, the United States Corps of Engineers built a breakwater. The objective was to protect the bay, not provide a new base for any so-called rebuilding of the town of Bayocean. To see Bayocean now and to compare it with when it was queen of Oregon coast resorts, is like looking at a once-beautiful woman to whom the years have been unkind.

The once-gracefully curved spit with its tall spectacular dunes covered with spruce, juniper and cedar trees, salal and Oregon Grape and a thriving community, is now just an unimaginative, vacant, graveled, windswept flatland which is held in place with beach grass, Scotch broom and a mass of wild strawberries. In 1989 the spit's major activity seems limited to horseback riding and beachcombing.

Bayocean was surely not the only place along the northwest coast to suffer erosion from the sea. Erosion has been documented along most of the Oregon and Washington shoreline but little of this is reported for a variety of reasons. Mainly, we presume, if nobody lives where it eroded, nobody cared. Some damages by the sea were not discovered for days after a washout.

What about Newport on the Lincoln County sea front? The town, a fishing village in early days, was huddled along the north shore of Yaquina Bay with a few summer homes perched on the cliffs over the hill and facing the ocean. During the 1912-1914 period, some houses "slipped" as the cliffs were apparently undermined during high winter tides. There were other "slips" in the early 1940s, then again forty years later.

There is Siletz Spit—commonly called Salishan Spit for the real estate development there. A few large substantial homes were built on the bluff at the base of the spit many years ago but assertive promotion to sell lots in the sand dunes that make up the spit apparently started in the mid-

1960s. The oceanographic disturbances at Salishan Spit are quite different from those that caused the erosion at Bayocean. At Siletz Bay there are no man-made "contrivances" (jetties) extending into the ocean which, as we shall see, caused the destruction of Bayocean. Nevertheless, Salishan lost its first house in January of 1973. A second, near the edge of the dune line, mysteriously burned a little later. Winter stormy seas beat down the high dunes along the spit causing many a front yard to disappear. In a few years, the once nearly 20-foot-high "cliff" became a sandy beach with a gentle slope to the sea. On at least two occasions since 1973, the ocean swept over the spit into Siletz Bay. The people who live there don't like to talk about it. But the spit has held to the present time.

A few years back the Oregon State Highway Department (now called the Department of Transportation) wanted to relocate Highway No. 101 to run along Nestucca Spit, which is a little south of Pacific City. Most of the spit south of the Nestucca River bridge at Pacific City is officially occupied by a state park, which is undeveloped except for a public boat launching ramp and car parking lot facing Nestucca River. Except for public rest rooms, there are no buildings in the park. Other than "politics," there seemed no reason why the highway couldn't be built there. Glad that it wasn't! In the winter of 1978, during a period of high tides and severe storms, an outer portion of the spit was leveled and, as with Bayocean, left the tip as an island. It appears to have been several days before anyone knew about it for, as indicated earlier, the outer spit was, and is at this writing, uninhabited.

In January 1983, winter storms again blasted and took off the end of the spit!

The Washington coast should not be left out. Cape Shoalwater is no more. North Cove is gone. For years the United States Coast Guard has been forced to relocate its Willapa Bay lighthouse several times, the most recent in summer 1988. Storms continue to lash the land at what is locally called "wash-away" beach. The town to the east, on a long hook, Tokeland, has been relatively safe. There is a village (North Cove) a little to the north of the prime erosion area, some of whose residents have cause to be nervous during winter storms due to the location of their places. There are isolated farms and a few homes in the "wash-away" area. These fall over the edge as the pounding surf beats at the dune.

The Washington Department of Fisheries, which maintains a watch along the shore, has detailed measurements of land losses over the years. "It's a continual mess," retorted Doug Simons of Fisheries during a discussion of coastal washouts in that area.

☆   ☆   ☆

The subject of erosion along the coasts of Oregon and Washington interested us years ago, so we brought out a thin book entitled *What Happened at Bayocean—Is Salishan Next?* in 1973. The public accepted the book well for it sold out within a few months. An expanded edition appeared the following year. This edition was also well received by visitors along the coast, and by librarians, as our book was the only one on the subject. When the book sold out in 1981, it was decided not to reprint for the obvious reason that "Salishan" was not next! Nestucca was.

In 1983 we presented a new book, *Maimed By the Sea*. That title again found high acceptance. When it became obvious that the book would soon sell out, we decided against reprinting for again, new material was uncovered. While other areas along the coast are covered here, the main story is Bayocean. Bayocean will probably be the main story until that day when the ocean's winter fury rips away Salishan. Geologists differ in the "guesstimates" when this will be.

Before the first World War, at a time when resort development was going on throughout the coastal areas of the United States, unless one had money to invest he probably didn't pay much attention to what real estate promoters were hawking. Unless one had invested in the Bayocean development, he probably gave little heed a few years later, to arguments between local port districts and the

Corps of Engineers.

Except for our research efforts and the present volume, the Bayocean story appears only in skimpy form in a few pages of a couple of books, and in some often inaccurate magazine articles and newspaper features. Some people we talked with want the matter forgotten, for they lost a lot of money out there, and said so in no uncertain terms. But these good folks are now pretty elderly or already gone. Others take a different view declaring, "It's history. Let's write it down!" And so we have.

Considering all the people who were heavily involved in Bayocean, three stand out. T. B. Potter, the investing developer; T. Irving Potter, who assumed much of the on-site management and advertising; Francis Drake Mitchell, the pharmacist and entrepreneur who bought the first lots. The Potters were promoters, movers and shakers. They did very well. T. B. Potter, as the developer, left his mark on history in several areas of the western United States but he will be most remembered for Bayocean.

"Mr. Mitchell," as he was called, lived at Bayocean longer than anyone else—about 45 years—so he knew more about the place including the politics.

Mitchell's private papers are few, probably going up in flames with his buildings when the area was officially cleared after the grand washout. Since 1972 we have personally visited, talked on the telephone, and exchanged letters with many people, with state and federal agencies and with indispensable reference librarians. Some of the folks whose help has been essential are remembered and thanked here. There are librarians from Missouri to southern California to northern Washington and of course several in Oregon. Richard Portal (now retired) helped get the research started. Karen Chase was involved a little later. Anne Billeter, the most recent, and her staff, at the Medford Main Branch of Jackson County Library System have been vital in this project.

M. Wayne Jensen, Jr., Director of Tillamook Pioneer Museum, has studied the subject of Bayocean and the museum holds a few artifacts from there. He has helped us willingly and often.

Gene and Lois Elliott, true Bayocean buffs, know nearly every inch of the place, have entertained us several times and assisted with this subject in a very real way.

We are indebted to the late Louis L. Bennett of Cape Meares, and to Howard "Buck" Sherwood, Bob and Barbara Watkins also of Cape Meares. Bennett and Sherwood spent much time hand drawing in locations of major buildings and the water works of Bayocean on a chart from the Corps of Engineers.

And Larry Coffelt, the present water manager at Cape Meares, said some of the original pipe and fittings are still in use. During a very recent chat at Cape Meares he mentioned, almost in passing, that he believed it was a descendant of T. B. Potter who had visited the area and wanted to "see his grandfather's lot." In a front yard conference between the authors, the Watkins' and Coffelt, at the Watkins' "pagoda" home, and with later input from Wayne Jensen, we were able to locate not one grandson but three! David T. Dobbins is living in Coronado, California. On a recent visit with Dr. John Potter Dobbins in San Marino, California, we together filled in earlier vacancies in our research and cleared up some "shadow" areas. Dr. Dobbins provided photographs of the late T. B. Potter and of T. Irving Potter that have eluded us for years. He, and his wife Violet ("Vi"), were cordial hosts and contributed greatly to this project. John Dobbins also put us in touch with Thomas Irving Potter, Jr., of Winslow, Washington. Thomas Potter provided the copy of *The Spectator* paper we have already quoted and supplied supporting evidence on several matters.

The Archivist of the City of Portland, Steve Webber, searched for early Potter interests in that city which included identification of Arleta sub-division as an early Potter project.

Dr. J. Kenneth Munford, Corvallis, now retired from his earlier position as Director of Oregon State University Press, has always had an interest in Bayocean and is one of those who contributed to this study, especially with encouragement.

Preface

Burford Wilkerson, William Finch, Hershal H. Stuart, the late Russell Hoover, Sr., Jean (Randall) Hopkins provided photographs to enhance our writing.

Dr. John Poulson Trommald, M.D., spent "decades of summers" on Bayocean starting in 1912 and related many of his experiences there to us. He also critically reviewed an earlier manuscript.

Leonard Lukens and Richard W. Helbock, postal historians; Thomas J. Murray, Port Consultant to cities of Bay City and Tillamook, were of specific help.

Our thanks go to many in the U.S. Corps of Engineers for their enthusiastic support with maps and aerial photos.

Herbert Schlicker, formerly with the State of Oregon Department of Geology and Mineral Industries, provided help by letters and interviews then looked over the original manuscript.

To our son Dale and his wife Sally, who made many trips to Bayocean, Salishan and to Nestucca, usually with camera, we thank you.

A friend indeed is Greta Forbish, long of Portland, but who spent many a summer (with family) starting in 1939 at Bayocean, then continued vacationing (still with family) at Oceanside after the washout at Bayocean.

She loaned many old photographs and classic cartoons she had drawn first on 1¢ then 2¢ then 3¢, 4¢ and finally on 5¢ postal cards—time and postage march on! Her recollections of vacations at Bayocean, and particularly her observations of the late Mr. and Mrs. Mitchell will be recorded here. In *Maimed By the Sea* we included five of her postal card drawings. When we talked with her recently she was so enthusiastic about the subject she did a few more drawings reflecting those earlier times specifically for this book. Greta, you are charming! We thank you.

Bert and Margie Webber   May 1989

About the Second Printing

In this Second Printing we have enlarged some pictures and changed a few where better views became available. The text remains the same thus this book is compatible with the earlier book.

Bert and Margie Webber   March 1992

13

Thomas Benton Potter (top) developer of Bayocean Park and his son Thomas Irving Potter who directed operations after his father became ill about 1910-1912.

CHAPTER 1

A GRAND NOTION

By 1906, Thomas Benton Potter was well established as a real estate promoter. He and H. L. Chapin, a surveyor, had platted and developed the Arleta (R-lee-tah) subdivision in Portland under the name Potter-Chapin Realty Company. Potter had by then finished his work on Arleta Park overlooking the Pacific Ocean at Half Moon Bay in

14

California. (Arleta was the name of his daughter.) He marketed the Marlborough Heights suburb on the south side of Kansas City, Missouri, and eventually owned it.

That Potter had money to spend as he wished there was no doubt. His developments were very profitable. He was a wealthy man. He traveled around the country in a private, specially outfitted Pullman car which he could hook to the fastest trains.

At Tillamook he observed a long, peaceful uninterrupted beach about four miles long that was 1,000 feet wide. Near the middle of the spit a huge tree-covered knoll rose to 140 feet. This peninsula was about 600 acres and at its widest was over half a mile. Potter, being a seasoned "possibility thinker," planned a resort community he believed would equal Atlantic City itself.

Potter and Chapin planned a great summer resort community. They chose the name Bayocean Park. His son, T. Irving Potter, had attend the Portland High School and later University of California. During summers his father took him to Kansas City where the young man became very proficient in real estate sales. As we shall see, it would be T. Irving Potter who did most of the promoting for Bayocean.

In the meantime, everything that concerned the building and the selling of Bayocean had to be developed. Sales pitches were planned. Brochures were printed. Construction on major attractions, at Potter's expense, had to be started. This meant hiring many workers as well as engineers and specialists. Potter and Chapin planned campaign trips and privately dreamed of making millions. But they had some challenges. Southern California property was being nationally advertised and was pulling a lot of investors. And just a few miles north of Bayocean Park was an Oregon coast community called "Seaside." Bayocean was a new name. Its location was off the beaten track. No one could know about it until the men got their promotions going. Seaside, on the other hand, was well known in Oregon history. Lewis and Clark established a salt cairn there in 1806. Settlers had arrived by 1850 and a post office, Seaside House, was in business in 1873. This became Sea Side in 1882, and one word, Seaside, in 1888. Neither Potter nor Chapin would ever utter the name "Seaside" in public for they were well informed of the resort plans there. They set out to promote Bayocean Park and they undertook some extraordinary means to do so.

Automobiles, a new fad, were certain to become popular so the promoters specifically planned to construct several miles of concrete "driveways" at their resort. Potter and Chapin would have to bring in fresh water, there being none on the spit, but was envisioned as a minor engineering inconvenience. The promotional campaign was developed in a step-by-step manner. As they planned, once prospective buyers arrived on the site, they would be wined and dined. Lulled with full stomachs, the promoters would start the pitch. They determined the best way to handle this would be to build a luxury hotel with all the trappings therefore, the first major project was to design a hotel and to get

Promoter T. B. Potter envisioned a grand hotel he planned to build at Bayocean atop the highest dune.

In addition to the luxury hotel, Potter planned a great Natatorium to "be built right on the beach." Architect's drawing faces east with proposed town of Bayocean in the background on Tillamook Bay.

newspaper editors to write about it. A real estate development of this magnitude would take a lot of time and lots of money. Potter advanced money but this was quickly gobbled up. Potter and Chapin needed to get potential buyers to their site very quickly so new money would start flowing in their direction. As it would take a long time to build their grand hotel, Potter started work immediately on an "annex" in which he would house his guests until the grand building was finished. He envisioned the "annex" would eventually be used to house the hotel's servants.

Potter was well aware of scientific advancements so played up telephones, electric lights and automatic fire sprinklers. His hotel would have them all.

The promoters realized they couldn't talk business every minute they had prospects on their spit, so they listed several "recreational" ideas. In the beginning the area was, they were fully aware, an open-air emporium of vacant sand dunes which they agreed would only be referred to as "building sites." The *elite*, at whom they were aiming, already played golf and tennis so they planned a course and courts. For the non-outdoor, but sporty type, they would advertise a natatorium—a great indoor swimming pool.

Potter learned that a motion picture theatre had opened in the east in the summer of 1905, had less than 100 chairs and netted over $1,000 a week. He believed he could attract a lot of people to his resort if he had a movie theatre. He decided to build one.

Potter immediately started to talk up his natatorium. It would be huge with a 160-foot pool and would be built right on the beach at the line of the first dunes. As water in most swimming pools just "lays there, motionless and uninteresting," Potter proclaimed that he would install electrically operated equipment to provide "artificial surf—so real in its action as to fool Old Neptune himself!"

Never once did Potter seem concerned about setting buildings on sand foundations.

Up to this point in Potter's planning, he did not mention how he expected people to get to Bayocean. There was no highway along the Northwest Coast. There was no road from Portland to Tillamook City. But he was quietly watching progress of the Pacific Railway & Navigation Company as it constructed its rail line from Portland to Tillamook. Did he envision parking his own private railroad car on a siding across from Bayocean and signing his juiciest deals in the car? But the depression of 1907 stopped work on the railroad. Frustration! He would have to come up with some other means. He decided to use the Columbia River!

But getting a ship which would handle well in the river as well as in the open sea was another matter. After considerable investigation in ports along the Pacific Coast as well as on the Atlantic side, quite a lot of time slipped by. In desperation, he contracted with R. A. Ballin, a ship designer in Portland, to design a motor yacht that would be suitable for the service he required. After approval, the plans were presented to Joseph Supple, who operated a shipyard on the Willamette River in Portland, with an order to build the ship. To get all possible publicity, Potter notified the newspapers of his plans for the yacht which he named *Bayocean*.

There was a lot of ship building on Portland's waterfront but this ship would be different. Potter proudly stated *Bayocean* was the largest motor passenger vessel built to that time (1911) on the Willamette River. In fact, he was to soon learn, his ship was the largest of its type to appear anywhere along the Pacific Coast. His goal for finding a method of getting monied prospects to his beach property was about to be achieved. He wanted a first class yacht and *Bayocean* would surely be that. The ship was 150 feet long with a beam of 18 feet. She mounted two raked funnels and had a clipper bow. One hundred passengers could be carried at a time—fifty in staterooms, first class of course, and fifty as day passengers on deck and in the men's smoking and reading cabin. Potter directed that his yacht be painted white.

Unidentified speaker at launching of *Bayocean* in Portland, where hundreds gathered to witness the event.

Bayocean

In 1910 T. B. Potter's health started to fail. His son assumed the position of operations manager. In most accounts, the dealing of the two Potters are merged leaving it unclear exactly where "T. B." stepped back, the "T. Irving" stepped in. They had been working together thus the transfer appears to have been without any notice. The yacht would be launched in 1911.

Until *Bayocean* was ready, the Potters leased other vessels.

M.V. Bayocean, **loaded with passengers and with flags and pennants flying, heads down Willamette River from Portland. The 150-foot long yacht, described as "magnificant" in the newspapers, was the largest private yacht on the Pacific Coast.**

On launching day, hundreds turned out jamming traffic and stalling trolley cars for blocks. The yacht was majestic. It had sleek, clean lines. On the stern Potter flew a huge American 46-star flag which stood straight out in the fresh breeze.

The first trip to Tillamook Bay on Bayocean was a great adventure which Potter had been vicariously enjoying for months. But when sailing day came, there is no evidence that T. B. Potter was on board. He was a sick man. But his son was there.

While details of the first trip defy documentation, the overall plan survives.

Family records indicate the gentleman in the front row, second from left, kneeling, is T. Irving Potter shown on the deck with "prospects" (except *Bayocean*'s Captain, in uniform) on the first trip.

Bayocean would sail down the Willamette from Portland in mid-morning and enter the Columbia River about an hour later. Potter was in no hurry. He wanted people on shore to see his beautiful ship and to inquire where it was going. At the peak of the mast was his pennant, "T. B. POTTER."

The first leg of the trip was about 100 miles to Astoria where he stopped whether there were passengers waiting or not. Again, Potter wanted and got publicity. His colossal, bright, new yacht was something to write about. Following castoff at Astoria, *Bayocean* made her way over the Columbia River bar and into the North Pacific Ocean.

We pause to consider: Nearly all of Potter's passengers were "landlubbers," some from mid-west states. It could be presumed at least some had been row-boating on ponds and lakes, and possibly in a river, but crossing the Columbia bar is something else. Potter does not seem to have ever warned his guests of possible seasickness, and maybe he just did not foresee this hazard. But we can be certain that some of his guests needed "resting time" once they arrived at their destination before they would be receptive to any sales pitch. Potter's grand hotel had not been started. His "annex" was still under construction so he rented all the rooms in Mitchell's Bayside Hotel which was next to the dock.

From his ship's skipper, Potter soon learned, if his stomach had not already made a personal announcement, that his grand yacht was somewhat cranky—unstable— while crossing not only the notorious, man-drowning Columbia River bar, but also while crossing the relatively easy bar at the entrance of Tillamook Bay.

Nevertheless, Potter provided a good show for those on board his yacht. The *Bayocean* headed out to sea after leaving the river, eventually circling close enough to the Columbia River Lightship for some passengers and lightship crewmen to exchange greetings with cardboard megaphones. This side trip was also an ingenious way to avoid allowing his passengers a peek of the coastal resort town of Seaside! On leaving the lightship, *Bayocean*'s skipper had a choice. He could cruise to Tillamook Rock Lighthouse for a look, or drive the ship straight for Tillamook Bay. On crossing that bar, the yacht made a grand circle, to avoid shallow water over mud flats, and entered a specially dredged channel for a straight run of the last few hundred yards to Potter's dock. Sometimes this voyage took two or three days. In the early days, T. B. Potter probably made a number of trips with his guests but for the most part he delegated the hosting and promotions to his partner, Chapin, and to his son. It's been suggested if Potter's (either one of them) hawking on board ship was successful, the skipper would slow the vessel's progress so deals could be closed without the interruption of landing, getting settled in the Bay Hotel, then cranking up the excitement for investing a second time.

T. Irving Potter was successful. Very successful. It was not long before he bought out Chapin. But he was always under pressure to find better ways to get more prospective

When the railroad finally started to operate, Potter tied up the *Bayocean* and chartered whatever number of seats he needed—sometimes entire cars—to bring "Prospects," in the guise of sight seeing tours, to his resort.

NEW LINE TO
BAYOCEAN

via the

Southern
Pacific

and
Pacific Railway
& Navigation Company
Commencing
Friday, Nov. 10, 1911

Trains will run daily, except
Sundays, as follows:

Lv. Portland ....7:20 A. M.
Lv. Hillsboro ....8:50 A. M.
Ar. Bay City (Bayocean Station)....1:45 P. M.
Ar. Tillamook ....2:25 P. M.

Lv. Tillamook ....7:55 A. M.
Lv. Bay City (Bayocean Station)....8:35 A. M.
Ar. Hillsboro ....1:25 P. M.
Ar. Portland ....4:10 P. M.

Tickets for sale at City Ticket Office, to
all points on P. R. & N.

Further particulars
JOHN M. SCOTT
General Passenger Agent, Portland

buyers to his resort and get them there quicker. He wanted a continuous stream of people rather than having to await round trips of his yacht. Thousands more would surely have come if there had been more convenient ways of getting there.

The Pacific Railway & Navigation Company was incorporated specifically for the purpose of hauling beach-bound vacationers from Portland to Tillamook County beaches. This was in 1905 and before the Potter's interest in the coast.

Much earlier, rail service had been opened from Portland, down the Columbia River to Astoria, thence south to Seaside. In railroad circles, some thought the tracks would extend on south to the Tillamook County beaches but this never materialized. Potter, on planning his strategy for getting people to his properties, was quite

R.L. POLK DIRECTORY—1907-8

BAYOCEAN PARK

AT TILLAMOOK BAY

The New Summer Resort

Potter - Chapin Realty Co., Inc.

OWNERS

402 COUCH BUILDING

109 Fourth Street   PORTLAND, OREGON

R.L. POLK DIRECTORY—1909

BAYOCEAN

AT TILLAMOOK BAY

The New Summer Resort

Potter-Chapin Realty Company, Incorporated

OWNER

514 CORBETT BUILDING

109 Fourth Street   PORTLAND, OREGON

R.L. POLK DIRECTORY—1910

BAYOCEAN

THE GREAT BEACH RESORT

AT TILLAMOOK BAY, 57 MILES DUE WEST OF PORTLAND.
$1,000,000 NOW BEING EXPENDED ON
IMPROVEMENTS AND ATTRACTIONS

POTTER-CHAPIN REALTY COMPANY

(Owner)

PORTLAND OFFICE, 514 CORBETT BUILDING.

R.L. POLK DIRECTORY—1911

OLK'S CLASSIFIED 1911 BUSINESS DIRECTORY   1709

•Beach Resorts

BAYOCEAN, TILLAMOOK BAY, 720 Corbett Bldg. (See Right Top Corner Cards and adv)

Bed Manufacturers

Holmes Disappearing Bed Co 422 Failing bldg

Bee Supplies

BAYOCEAN

BEACH SEASON 1911.

OREGON'S $1,000,000 SUMMER PLAYGROUND

HOTEL ANNEX AND TENT CITY

For Rates and Literature, HOTEL BAYOCEAN ANNEX, BAYOCEAN, OREGON

pleased to learn that the P.R. & N. wanted to serve beach traffic in his neighborhood and had no interest in Seaside.

While the casual observer would probably not be aware of the rivalries between developers, the fellows promoting Seaside did not care for the "upstart—Potter," whom they discovered was diverting potential investors away from Seaside. These developers believed they saw in the P.R. & N., the equivalent of a railroad being run almost exclusively for the benefit of Potter's building lot promotion scheme at Bayocean. These promoters fumed but they were powerless to do anything about it. Young Potter had class. They didn't. Potter was flamboyant. His dad paraded around the railroads in his private car. (See appendix) The Seaside developers didn't have any of this. Potter was aggressive and downright brash at times. The only reason Potter built his yacht was because the railroad wasn't ready for him. Potter was notably "testy" when rail construction came to a halt as a result of the 1907 depression, but not for long: He built the yacht. Potter, with his yacht, and later with "my railroad" as he sometimes called the P.R. & N., was surely diverting business away from Seaside. The ship was ready in 1911 and so was the railroad. Just how many trips *Bayocean* made has not been determined, but once the trains were running, the yacht was tied up. (See Appendix)

When the railroad opened late in 1911, Potter could charter cars, or entire trains if need be, to carry his prospects for a pittance compared to the cost of running his yacht. And of course the trip by rail was merely hours compared to days on the ship.

To complete our narrative about the railroad, it should be pointed out that one riding between Portland and Tillamook County passed over tracks of two railroads. Southern Pacific went into Portland from its Willamette Valley route plus what one today might call a "commuter" line to Beaverton via Oswego (Lake Oswego). Beach passengers from Portland purchased tickets on S.P. and had a choice. They could board a steam train and keep the seat all the way to the beach, or they could leave Portland half an hour later in the electric interurban arriving in Beaverton half an hour earlier than the steamer. Those who chose to ride the electric had to transfer to the steam train at Beaverton which went on to Hillsboro—end of the S.P. line. The Southern Pacific's engine was uncoupled and an engine of the P.R. & N. was hooked on for the trip to the beach. On return, the procedure was reversed.

The train, which was named "The Tillamook Flyer," didn't "fly" very fast. Its 91 miles of track went through sharp curves, over high trestles and through tunnels. Along the way it made thirty-four stops, finally arriving at Bay City, where Bayocean passengers detrained and took a ferryboat across Tillamook Bay to their destination. If all went well, the train ride between Portland and Tillamook was about seven hours!

Potter's weekend excursion trains cost just the price of the seats at $5.57 per adult round trip. After the railroad opened, the senior Potter, with his wife Mary Frances, had their own "cottage" there. (John Potter Dobbins describes his grandmother, "mater" as she was called, as a pert 4-foot 7-inches tall, well rounded "and did not weigh even 100 pounds when soaking wet.") When "T. B." was in residence, he met his guests at the terminal in Bay City then rode with them across the bay on a ferryboat.

One might conclude that Potter's dreams were being realized with the advent of the train but not so. Both Potters were never satisfied with the numbers of people they could draw even in this manner. And costs were running very high.

The Potters were capable of putting on tours and closing deals seven days a week—whenever they could get an audience. Although some of his guests bought building lots, most did not. It became the fashion of some folks to spend weekends as "prospects" at one resort then another on the pretense of having interest in purchasing property. For the most part, promoters paid round-trip transportation, some entertainment and many meals as well as free hotel accommodations. Accordingly, Potter needed more and more people to offset those who partook of his hospitality but bought nothing. He was good at cooking up publicity—lots of it. With the publicity came free-loaders in droves. He found it nearly impossible to place restrictions on whom he invited fearing to do so might run off real prospects.*

The transportation problem bothered Potter like a festering sore. It seemed to eat at the very foundation of his plans—and his potential profits—but he kept plugging with a never-say-die attitude. Despite the national depression of 1907 his enterprise had gotten off to a very firm start. With energetic advances in most every direction, including the Kansas City area, Potter worked his "connections." Scanty records suggest about 2,000 people came by invitation and paid out hundreds of thousands of dollars in a very short time. Even so, Potter was obsessed with an uncommon drive to bring in more people. Automobiles were becoming popular and it was the beginning of the national road-building era. If people could "motor" to his resort, Potter believed, he would not have to depend on others—boats, trains—to bring people to him. They could come on their own at their own expense.

Leave it to Potter to come up with a better plan! He announced a "tour package." Selected groups would be allowed to *pay* for spending a weekend on the spit! We will discuss this in a later chapter.

Unfortunately, a road to Bayocean was many years away. The senior Potter would not live to see it. By the time the road was in, the younger Potter would be out of the real estate game and following an unrelated career in the east.

Even without a road, people flocked to Bayocean as fast as they could be accommodated. Potter pushed work on the hotel's annex. □

*The authors accepted an invitation to "tour" a condominium north of Newport, on the Oregon Coast in 1987 to check out the "deal." The promise, for those who gave about two hours to the salesman, was a $20 bill in the hand at the close of the presentation.

CHAPTER 2

WATER FOR
A WATERLESS TOWN

When the resort was still in the planning stage, T. B. Potter hired an engineer, Mr. C. E. Lockwood. According to a newspaper clipping, Lockwood was responsible for the general plat of the town and for a municipal water system. Lockwood went to the spit for study.

In a short time he recognized three potential sources for "city water." He could drill wells but each well would require a pump house. Pumps would require either steam or electricity for operation. While there were trees in abundance on Kincheloe Point, the northern end of the spit which faced the entrance to the bay, Lockwood was of the opinion these should be left standing for non-commercial use. He reported that steam operated pumps would have to operate almost 24-hours a day once the town was populated. If steam engines had to be used, he declared that Potter would have to build a road to Cape Meares where Potter would then have to set up and operate a logging camp on a near-continuous basis. This in addition to having to import fairly heavy trucks. The trucks would be a continuous matter of maintenance. He would have to build a garage, buy parts, and hire a full-time mechanic. Too expensive!

Another idea for a water supply was Lockwood's realization that the north Oregon coast had plenty of rain which might be collected and stored in cisterns. With a geologist, Lockwood hiked through the timber and underbrush seeking locations for his cisterns. During their exploration, they discovered several springs. Why not tap the springs? If the springs didn't produce enough water year around, he could always build the cisterns and use them as backup. He decided on the springs as best. They seemed the

F. D. Mitchell, who bought first tract, quickly built Bayshore "Bay" Hotel (top and center) then Mitchell Bldg. (center right and bottom) Sign: "This Place Will Be Occupied by Mitchell & Baker, Real Estate."

most dependable and the quickest and easiest to adapt for the least expense. Potter liked the idea and directed Lockwood to proceed.

(As yet there was no electricity on the site although Potter had told Lockwood that Lockwood would eventually be asked to plan for lighting the major buildings. But a water works was the highest priority. Potter advertised he would provide "paved driveways" and water was a must for mixing mortar.)

Lockwood's water works was ingenious! He devised a gravity system that originated from a spring high on Cape Meares. The spring fed Coleman Creek. Lockwood diverted this small creek into a holding tank that was about 10-feet square. The tank was concrete. From the tank he ran tar covered wood pipe of from six to eight inch diameter down the cape to near sea level. The pipe made a turn to the west then another turn north at the neck of the spit. It then followed the bay side of the spit to the town site. At intervals he installed "T" joints from which the line would serve various parts of town. At a point near the center of the town, Lockwood's water line went up the side of a 140-foot high dune on top of which would be Potter's fashionable hotel.

Lockwood explained to Potter that pressure from the drop down the side of Cape Meares, five miles or so south, would be enough to deliver fresh drinking water to the hotel as well as to way points. Lockwood built the system. It worked.

Limited records do not reveal details of the early operations of this "Water Department," but Swan Hawkinson operated the works for years. After World War II, the Water Board was made up of Jack Gillham, Barney Randall and Russell E. Hoover. Hoover was superintendent only because (as he wrote in 1973) he owned 42 cabins in Cottage Park "and it was to our own benefit that I take over the superintendency of the water line." These men moved following the 1948 washout. Hoover continued, "We sold out our interest in the cabins in 1949 as most of the people had left by then. After we sold out and there was little left,

T. B. POTTER
REALTY
COMPANY

Originator, Designer and Owner of *Oregon's* newest, biggest and best Summer Resort on Tillamook Bay and the Pacific Ocean.

Bayocean

Nearest seaside playground to the Northwest and accessible by rail, steamer, automobile, stage or horse back

General Offices: 720 Corbett Building
PORTLAND, OREGON

This advertisement ran in Potter's paper, *The Surf*. He was a big thinker and followed his ideas with actions. (Right) Rock crushing equipment was inside barn-like building on narrow, south portion of spit. When spit washed out near here the breach was called "Rock Crusher Gap." (Bottom) Three palatial homes built on top of the 140-foot high dune near hotel. Hicks' house on right, where six-inch well casing was sunk, is one of six houses moved from the spit before final breaching. Picture was probably made from an upper story window of the hotel.

the Water Board met and disbanded the Bayocean Water District and turned it over to Louis Bennett.'' Bennett was a carpenter who arrived at Bayocean during World War II. (He helped construct blimp hangars still seen south of Tillamook.) When the authors talked with Bennett in early 1973 he related, ''I still lived on Bayocean then and had a nice house which earlier was owned by the Campfire Girls organization. If I was to have water at my place somebody had to step forward to 'tend the system' so I did it.'' In the 1970s Bennett could remember where every line had been and where the controlling valves were. At that time some of Lockwood's original pipes were still serving an area south of the original peninsula (part now under the sea) known as Ocean park. Today this general area is called the Cape Meares Community. In 1978 Larry Coffelt became ''water manager.'' In 1989 he told us that a few parts of the old system were still serving the community.

Because of lack of use of some lines, Bennett told of his having to flush the pipes in order to maintain fresh water. He related that at times ''the water smelled awful, but nobody ever got sick from it.'' He recalled the pressure was a problem. At the bottom of the run down the steep hill pressure was nearly 100 pounds. There seems to have been at least one court case of complaint against the water company in which a water patron claimed the pressure was too much. But the pressure on the line by the time the gravity flow climbed the 140-foot high hill out on the spit was ''sometimes troublesome,'' again quoting Bennett. C. G. Hicks, who had a large home on the hill, needed more water than the system could deliver. He decided to drill a well. The bore for his well was not difficult for there was only sand to penetrate—140 feet of it to sea level—then a little deeper until he struck fresh water. He sank a 6-inch cast-iron pipe the entire distance. Bennett related when the well was nearly finished, something went wrong which caused a break and admitted sea water. Unperturbed, Hicks, Bennett said, placed a 3-inch pipe within his 6-inch casing. Hicks then attached a hand pump which, after priming, delivered all the fresh water he wanted.

Erosion took the 140-foot high dune, leaving Hicks' well—the 6-inch pipe (top left) 1959 view, (top right) in 1972. (Bottom) May 1981. 3-inch core within 6-inch pipe. Margie inspects at low tide. Pipe was unchanged on Jan. 30, 1983. A little less of it remained in June 1986. When the authors were on the spit April 30, 1989, no trace of the pipe could be found.

Years later, over a period of time, the angry sea knocked down that 140-foot high sand dune and most of the buildings that were perched on top of it. This included Potter's hotel "annex." (Due to lack of money and circumstances in which he found himself, including law suits, his grand hotel was never built.)

Hicks' well collapsed as the dune disintegrated. A picture was made of the remains of the well casing in 1959, then nearly one-quarter of a mile at sea at high tide. At that time about ten feet of pipe was shown sticking out of the beach at low tide. A close look reveals that the pipe was broken at a joint. It is obvious, by looking closely at the picture, there is something inside the 6-inch pipe holding it in place. The 3-inch insert? By 1972, when the authors photographed the pipe, it was considerably shorter and visible only at low tide.

Winter storms continued to pound and the pipe, continuing to rust, broke again. In 1981, with only about 12 inches remaining above the beach at very low tide, the authors walked out to the pipe and made closeup photographs. The pictures very clearly validate Bennett's story of a 3-inch pipe being inside the 6-inch casing.

The decision to drill a well came years before "permits" and before ecological considerations were weighed to what effect, if any, such drilling might have on sand dune stabilization. Did the presence of the well contribute to the fall of the sand dune into the sea? Not likely, say geologists.

Lockwood's decision to tap the springs as his source of water for Bayocean, and now the Cape Meares Community, seems to have been a good one. □

(Opposite) Trees cleared, top of 140-foot high dune ready for hotel construction for which Bayocean railroad would haul supplies. (Top to bottom) Completed, hotel was luxurious, included telephones—note switchboard—electric lights. By 1940 only shell remained as the dune and building fell into the sea. In World War II, shell housed Coast Guard patrol war dogs.

CHAPTER 3
CONSTRUCTION BEGINS

Engineer Lockwood platted the town carefully. Because Potter had advertised concrete streets, Lockwood drew them in, then set about to have construction superintendent M. J. O'Donnell lay them. O'Donnell needed fresh water for his concrete batch plant. There was plenty of sand right on the beach and for rock, that too could be scooped from a rocky area of the beach. All Potter needed to import was sacked cement, rock crushing equipment and a mixer. But there was still another consideration. When one needs to haul heavy loads and there are no trucks or roads, the thing to do is build a railroad. O'Donnell did just that. He ordered what is believed to have been a brand new Vulcan locomotive plus several 4-wheel flat cars. While the engine was on order he planned his system. He would lay 21-pound "light" rail on ties for a 30-inch gauge line. The track would run from the dock up the hill to the hotel site and with a switch, to the concrete batch plant and rock crusher on the narrow end of the spit. The track would be highly portable with ties resting on the sand. When a building project was completed in one area, men would pick up the track in sections then place the sections where they wanted to run the train next. Potter would proclaim his development had the largest payroll in Tillamook County. He was probably right.

His little train, officially known as "The Bayocean Railroad," but affectionately dubbed "The Dinky," hauled rock, sand, lumber, kegs of nails, barrels of oil, and everything else which was required to build a town. He did not envision that his train would be used for "joy riding," but as we shall see, it was used for that too. It must have been an interesting spectacle to watch the little engine chug up the 12th Avenue hill pulling toy-size flat cars loaded with

(From top):
Natatorium on
beach's edge.
Dance Pavilion
in trees, one of
few buildings
destroyed by
fire. Guests at
resort trudge
through sand
near Tent City.

building materials during the week, but loaded with "guests" who enjoyed the "joy ride" on weekends.

When the streets were eventually finished, there were about three and one-half miles of paving. O'Donnell's rock crusher let many goose-egg-sized cobbles slip through, these ending up as bumps in the pavement, no two exactly alike.

Up the hill at the hotel, a telephone switchboard was installed behind the room-clerk's desk. Nobody seemed to mind that the system did not go anywhere except around the town. Years later a hefty twist on the crank raised "central" in Tillamook, who could plug through to Portland.

O'Donnell put in a diesel engine to operate a power plant, thus the hotel, natatorium, other buildings and some homes whose owners wanted to buy the service, could get electricity. The "wave machine" at the "nat" was also

"Tent City" which had been set up to accommodate the construction workers, was a "low rent" district for "guests" who did not afford hotel rooms. Each tend had a wood stove and a few were wired for electric lights. "Street lights"—bare light bulbs—dangled from the overhead wires.

electrical. The natatorium had a wood-fired boiler to provide hot showers as well as to take the sea-chill off the pool's water.

Potter collected fancy prices for fancy lots, as high as $1,800. A "fancy" lot faced the ocean, was on a paved street, was served by his water system so had "inside plumbing." Potter planned these to be along the route of his pole line on which the electricity would be available. Others, who took land farther back paid much less, as low as $200. These did not have water and were on "graded" laterals to the paved driveways.

Potter wanted cash up front when he could talk his "guests" into taking clear title immediately. He wanted to be able to hawk how many lots had been sold. He also needed money to keep up his development projects. His "deals" were made to fit the individual case. To those who wanted property in his resort but were low of cash, he would take a down payment and provide a time-pay contract. As we shall see, all his deals were not as "pure" as he advertised.

The first person of record to buy lots was Francis Drake Mitchell. He was a druggist, age 37. Mitchell was a fellow of great enthusiasm and stamina and he would spend the greater part of his life at Bayocean.

As part of his plans for entertaining his guests, Potter asked Lockwood to design a huge dance pavilion near the "nat." This was an open-air affair. That is, it had a roof but all sides were exposed to the weather. After the first few months of huffing and puffing of chilly and often rainy blasts, which forced Saturday night dancers into heavy coats, the Bayocean Commercial Company (headed by Potter) installed heavy canvas curtains on the seaward side. Potter hired dance orchestras from distant cities for special weekend promotions.

Some said the dance hall fell into the sea later, caused by coastal erosion, however, some evidence reveals the pavilion burned down after a frivolous weekend of partying. One feature Potter's town did not have was a fire department. □

T. B. Potter's residence at Bayocean was up the hill, west of the dock. One had to pass his residence to get to the dance hall, the natatorium or the hotel from the dock. In the picture observe the extentions on the chimneys which allowed better draw for his fireplace and for the kitchen woodstove.

Potter imported a brass band from Portland to play for Bayocean's Grand Opening, Saturday, June 22, 1912.

CHAPTER 4

EARLY PROGRESS

Potter's publicity paid off well for Bayocean became known as a gala place. The business district of the community was near the dock and took on a carnival atmosphere for the Grand Opening on Saturday, June 22, 1912. For this event Potter imported a brass band from Portland. The band played marches to everyone's delight in the town center, then the band marched up Twelfth Avenue and over Laurel Street to the hotel for a noon concert. That night the Bayocean Commercial Club, which had followed Potter's nudging, put on a huge fireworks display from atop the high dune near the hotel while the band played more stirring marches. The display of pyrotechnics was seen as far away as Tillamook City across the bay.

By now another corporate name appeared, the Bay-ocean-Tillamook Company, which, as expected, T. Irving Potter operated.

In "downtown" Bayocean, merchants were busy and

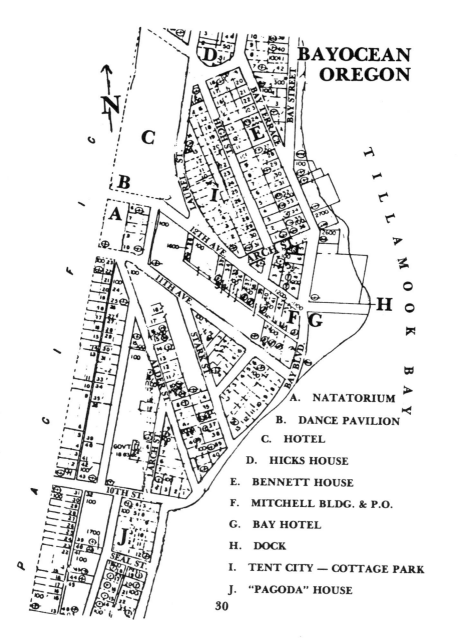

BAYOCEAN
OREGON

A. NATATORIUM

B. DANCE PAVILION

C. HOTEL

D. HICKS HOUSE

E. BENNETT HOUSE

F. MITCHELL BLDG. & P.O.

G. BAY HOTEL

H. DOCK

I. TENT CITY — COTTAGE PARK

J. "PAGODA" HOUSE

30

happy. In addition to a well-stocked general store with Post Office—which postmarked outgoing mail "BAYOCEAN, OREG." with a hand canceler—there was a trap-shoot range and a bowling alley. Potter's tennis courts near the hotel were always busy but he never did put in the golf course. What today might be called a "rock-hound" headquarters—an agate shop—opened. Tillamook County beaches, particularly Bayocean's, were noted for very large agates. (Mary Potter was a beachcomber. She collected seashells and agates of every local variety.) Potter's official office was in Portland where most of his one-man think-tanking was done, but he also maintained a residence and office at the resort. When the development was fairly well along after the trains were running, he lived at the beach most of the time. When his plans were firm for staying at the beach full time, his wife fitted their brand new home on Bay Terrace for winter use.

Potter was a dreamer who set his immediate and long-range goals carefully, then made the effort to achieve them. He believed in communicating. He bought lavish advertising space in the papers and created his own newspaper which he called *The Surf*. He published it monthly. The authors have determined that the first issue probably appeared in November 1911. His was a quality-printed, 4-page, coated sheet as opposed to ordinary newsprint. He used photo-engravings of people, buildings and series pictures showing construction progress. Single copies were 5¢ but he probably gave many away. The April 1912 edition was 8 pages. The paper promoted the resort, the town, and the new Port District which was created following a vote of the people who lived there. The paper contained news of the Tillamook vicinity including stories about planned improvements to be made to the Tillamook Bar. An item has F. D. Mitchell, the druggist, Lockwood, the engineer, and others on a commit-tee of the Bayocean Commercial Club working with the Tillamook City Chamber of Commerce to promote a County Fair.

The Surf contained advertisements, both display and classified, many of which were Potter's. But merchants at the resort also supplied the paper with ads as did some outside business houses. In one edition there is a full-page advertisement for *The Book of Knowledge* encyclopedia. To claim *The Surf* was "all Potter ballyhoo" would not be accurate.

Bayocean had a tin shop and a machine shop, both needed for developing the resort. It has been said that the tinner, who lived in "Tent City" which had been developed for the workers, spent much of his spare time hand making models of the yacht from scraps. These models, between 12 and 18 inches long, were sold to visitors and became highly prized novelties in later years. The Bayocean Bakery was a busy place because bustling bakers busily baked biscuits, beans, beautiful buttery banana buns and blueberry bread for the benefit of the beach community. There were several small cafes and of course the Bayshore Inn, generally just called the Bay Hotel, near the dock. There was a swimming pool about which very little is known. It was an open-air pool and was called the Bay Plunge. According to articles in *The Surf*, it was at the foot of Alder Street at Bay Blvd.

Mary Frances Potter (center) with friends in front of the cubicle dressing rooms at Bay Plunge.

THE SURF

Vol. I No. 3   BAYOCEAN, OREGON, JANUARY 1, 1912   Monthly

| 1912 | ## Foreword | 1912 |

THE Christmas has come and gone, and it is to be hoped that it was a merry one for all.

The New year has arrived, it looks to us like a healthy youngster and we are willing to do our share in seeing it grow thru its youth, prime and old age.

Our share in this will be as always, the giving of information to those interested in the development of Bayocean.

This information will be based on the facts as they exist, not as we would like to see them, but as they really are.

We want your support; we need it. You know Bayocean, you realize its future as you do its present worth.

Talk about it, give expression to some of the thoughts that come from knowing it. The beauties of this spot will appeal to others as it has appealed to you.

The development of Bayocean, as planned and being carried out to the last detail, means that city will arise, comparing favorably with Atlantic City.

The environments of Bayocean, natural and social, are unequaled; it logically becomes the natural selection for those seeking health, for those desirous of pleasure and society; as an investment, its advantages are apparent to the layman as well as the engineer and capitalist.

As a homesite, with woodland, ocean or bay to choose from as the mood dictates, but what the use, you have all seen it, or are going to see it, besides, we are not words artists, we leave the veneer of words to those who have something to cover, after all, it is apparent to those who know that nothing more can be said than

'IT IS BAYOCEAN.'

Saying that — comparisons are odious.

A view of sidewalk and street conditions on which fronts the bungalow of Mrs. T. B. Potter.

ASSURANCE OF FUTURE

Tillamook Bay Predestined to Reap Advantages of Panama Canal

Comparatively speaking, no one spot on the Pacific Coast will reap as many advantages by the opening of Panama as will Tillamook Bay.

As noted in our last issue, an organization, making it a public enterprise, has perfected the Port of Bayocean.

Efforts—with assurances of success—will result in the co-operation of the War Department to make this one of the safest of deep water harbors between San Francisco and the Columbia River.

With the assurance of service from all points thruout the Gulf and South Atlantic seaboard points by rapid and economical steamships, the Pacific Coast resorts are destined to become the Mecca of all tourists, instead of the European goals now sought by seekers of rest and recreation, as well as social mingling.

Nowhere in the Northwest can the 'elights of social intercourse be enjoyed as at Bayocean.

No spot anywhere in the land offers

DIRT FLYING AT BAYOCEAN

Street Work For December Ahead of November

The streets of Bayocean as seen by the visitors who have been there before, will be one big surprise on the next trip.

Chief Engineer Lockwood, with Supt. M. J. O'Donnell, have certainly been doing things in December.

High Street is now graded in its entirety and is ready for paving.

That portion of Pine Street from Birch to 16th Avenue is also in the same condition.

Alder Street is another on which the graders have finished with their part of the work, and as it looks—even now—the beauties of this thorofare appeal to all who have seen it.

Clark Street is well under way and shows completion of grades from Alder to 9th Avenue.

Then 16th Avenue is also ready for the paving from Park to Water, tho none will be laid until this street is graded its entire length.

Water Street from 16th to 17th has seen the last of the grading gangs

BAY CITY TO HAVE MODERN FACTORY

Bayocean Extends Best Wishes

BAY CITY, Or.—A car of new machinery has arrived for the Central Sash, Door & Manufacturing Company and a crew of men is busy installing it. The additional machinery places the equipment of the factory in such position that a strong bid for business can be made. W. M. Heacock, manager of the company, returned last week from a business trip to Portland, where he secured the additional Portland capital in the enterprise. The factory will begin operations soon after the first of the year with a large force of men.

STILL ANOTHER BOAT FOR BAY- OCEAN.

A. D. Chase, of Portland, and George Yale, of Bay City, have taken over the gasoline carrier "Osprey."

This is now in service between Portland to Tillamook Bay, Nestucca and Nehalem

Southern Pacific Railroad printed this advertising brochure in its efforts to sell excursions to Bayocean in 1913.

"Cottage Park" which replaced "Tent City," was mainly for transients and vacationers. Area was behind large dune, protected from ocean winds. In time, entire area shown would be under the sea. (Below) "Pagoda" houses were moved from spit to become a private residence in Cape Meares Community.

It was not long before there were year-round residents. As mentioned, some homes had electric lights from the central power plant. Others used kerosene and candles. Homes were generally heated by fireplaces or with wood-burning cook stoves. In the early days there was plenty of scrub timber for fuel at the north end of the spit—Kincheloe Point. In fact, there was a very good looking cabin built entirely of driftwood. Hot water came from two sources. The most common was from a pot on a cook stove. The other was from water pipes run through fire places and/or

APPLICATION FOR INFORMATION

T. B. POTTER REALTY COMPANY
720 Corbett Building
Portland, Oregon

Gentlemen:-

Will you kindly furnish me with an estimate of the cost, per person, for an excursion which includes the various features which I have checked below, with the understanding that I am not placed under any obligations to you, other than to present the matter to the organization for which I enquire, at the first meeting following your reply.

(a) The number in our party will be approximately .... people.

(b) We can spend about .... days in making the entire trip outlined below.

(c) We can make the trip, to the best advantage on or about ....

Following are the features we would like to have included in the trip, each one of which we have checked. Kindly forward an estimate of the cost, including all expenses, from the time of leaving Portland to return.

Genuine Kodak Outing ....
A dip in the surf at Bayocean ....
Private dance in the dancing pavilion ....
A still water swim in Tillamook Bay ....
Near view of 50 miles of Oregon Coast ....
A "joy ride" on the Bayocean Railroad ....
One day's stop at the Astoria Centennial ....
A day trout fishing in the mountain streams ....
Trip to the end of the Columbia River Jetty ....
One hundred miles down the Columbia River ....
Close view of the Columbia River Lightship ....
One night camping out in the wilds of the forest ....
A tramp up the beach to the Tillamook Bay Bar ....
A reception by the Tillamook Commercial Club ....
Close view of the warning light at Tillamook Rock ....
A bonfire and clam-bake on the beach in the evening ....
A walk through the famous forests of Tillamook timber ....
A jaunt to the Wind Caves at the lower end of Bayocean ....
A typical Pacific Ocean sea-food dinner at the Hotel Bayocean ....
Round the whistling buoy, marking Entrance to Tillamook Bay ....
A day visiting the canneries and saw mills along Tillamook Bay ....
A day on the ocean, including the kingly sport of deep sea fishing ....
A tramp to the Life Saving Station, including exhibition by the men ....
A visit to the dairy ranches and cheese factories of Tillamook County ....
A day in the wilds of the mountains on Cape Mears, with picnic lunch ....
A ride on the P. R. & N. Company's new railroad, Tillamook to Mohler ....
A trip to the top of Cape Mears, including visit to the Cape Mears Lighthouse ...
An exhibition of diving and fancy swimming by Arthur Cavill, world's champion ......
A moonlight picnic on the waters of Tillamook Bay, including luncheon and music ....

Signed ....

Official Title ....

Organization ....

Address ....

This form for Potter's "fee basis" tours was apparently good at least in late summer 1911 for the "stop at Astoria Centennial" was a pageant that played from Aug. 10 through Sept. 9 of that year.

the stoves. Those wanting a hot bath may have been faced with a challenge for there is no mention of any bathtubs, other than in the hotel, in the earlier years. Some homes on the spit were tied into the sewer which ran from the hotel through the main part of the business area, then to the end of the dock and dumped into the bay. Other homes were served by the time-honored privy. The natatorium, being on the beach was below the elevation needed to be hooked to the sewage drainage line. It appears to have been the only building equipped with a septic tank. Its drain field was the beach!

In the early days of his promotion, Potter hosted hundreds at his expense. As his resort took shape, he encouraged groups to make planned excursions to Bayocean for which each person would pay fees. This included entire families for he wanted people living there year round.

His manner of promoting group excursions was to approach an organization's secretary then hand that person his "Application for Information." This application was in the form of a letter which very clearly but nicely informed its readers such an excursion would cost money. He made it clear that the secretary was under no obligation "other than to present the matter to the organization for which I [the secretary] enquire at the first meeting following your reply" of costs. Then followed a list of 29 options. These ran from swimming in the surf to a "joy ride" on the Bayocean Railroad. Groups would decide what activities they wanted to pursue and would indicate how many days their excursion would be and when they wanted to go. All this would be "coordinated" in Potter's Portland office. His reply to the group was a statement of expenses from the time of leaving Portland to return.

Potter soon began to witness more business from the paid excursions than from his former all-expense paid trips. Could it have been that people who paid hard cash for something looked closer at Potter's investment opportunity than those who went for the "free ride"? The group excursion deal was offered before the trains were operating so all transportation was on the yacht. With sales booming, he continued the excursions for a while after the trains started.

Surfing was a great sport—and free other than rental of the boards. The beach was long and it was broad. Beachcombing on the high tides was always rewarding, especially in the winter months, and just laying on the beach and frolicking in the surf and on the sand was great sunny-day fun. For "day" visitors who did not have hotel rooms, a fellow built a long row of "dressing rooms" near the Bay Plunge. For a small fee, one could change into or out of a swim suit. A gent who recalled the cubicle rooms complained of their smallness and inability for both he and his girl friend to fit at the same time. He complained at having to rent two dressing rooms and paying two fees!

Boys and girls fished for crabs, boiled them over a beach fire then sold them to visitors "two-for-a-quarter." A favorite sport was to hunt rabbits. Kids could rent a .22 rifle. Rabbits could be found in the woods atop Kincheloe Point and in the lowlands at the spit's base. The bay was noted for its quality clams and on minus tide days people came from miles around just to go clam digging. If one did not own a boat he could rent one for a day's bay fishing. When Dr. John Poulsen Trommald was a boy, he said a fellow in Bay City designed a rowboat just for him, then rented it to him for an entire summer. Fishing was very good.

Almost from the start there was a small custom cannery at the resort which catered to visiting fishermen who could rent accommodations in Tent City. In time, the tents gave way to more permanent accommodations when a contractor was hired to roof and wall them in. This project gained the name "Bungalow City." The name later reduced simply to "Cottage Park."

Even though Potter was a hard driver in a situation that seems to have been one of continual stress, his hundreds of sales brought a certain degree of satisfaction. By 1914 he had sold over 1,600 building lots, had collected close to $600,000 and had another $300,000 on the books.

His stress was clearly that he needed more people to see

what he offered. But he could only haul so many on the yacht. With the train he got more but they came mostly on weekends with many freeloaders. All he needed was a road. (Bob Watkins, who has lived his life at Cape Meares Community, related in 1989 how, in the early 1920s, he would go with his mother and dad to Tillamook City on a raft every six weeks for supplies.) Part of engineer Lockwood's assignment was to lay out a road from Tillamook City. By this time, however, Potter's money was about used up and legal challenges were cropping up. It would be 1928 before a road materialized. In the meantime the few cars that enjoyed putt-putting around his "driveways," had to be boated to Bayocean so relatively few people bothered. The only vehicles permanently on the resort to the author's knowledge, were one car and one truck. Both were owned by Potter.

Potter had success, but with success came many challenges. Promises he made and promises of others were not always honored. While some disagreements could be either argued or pacified away, others went to court. The authors have not found evidence that T. B. or his son T. Irving sued anyone for failure to pay for a site. Plausibly this was because they would get the land back on a foreclosure anyway. The senior Potter had pretty well terminated his activities by 1912 when he retired to Alameda, California, due to bad health. By 1914, some evidence suggests that his son had either sold the realty company or just pulled out. He had other interests.*

The realty company was ordered into court by at least one dissatisfied customer.

Frank C. McNurlen, a young engineer working for the Oregon, Washington Railroad and Navigation Company, bought a parcel of land based on assertions of the T. B. Potter Realty Company. McNurlen bought the land with the understanding it was in the center of the growing business

---

*T. Irving Potter was an inventor of delicate machinery and founded The Coin Machine Company in Portland. Later, he headed the Patent Equity Association in New York City.

section of Bayocean, that it was close to the new dock and that streets were paved on all sides. When the fellow journeyed to the spit to look at his property he was distressed to discover that his site was in a stretch of sand dunes and brush, there were no near neighbors and the lot nearly inaccessible. He sued Potter for the cost of the lot, $525.00, as well as for $80.00 in expenses in going to look at the lot.

The Portland *Oregonian* edition of February 11, 1915, page 8, reported the matter:

> Gentlemen, there isn't an honest thing in this case excepting the hard dollars this engineer boy [McNurlen] earned working for the O.W.R. & N. Company and that these people stole from him. That is the plain English of it.

Circuit Judge McGinn, in deciding the case against T. B. Potter Realty Company who had sold the lot in Bayocean Park to McNurlen on allegedly false representations, awarded the young man full amount paid, including expenses for the inspection trip, and then stated:

> Photographs and pictures of Bayocean were turned over to this boy for one purpose, and that was to catch the unwary, those who were not posted, those who were not informed. It was done to fool him. It was done to catch him. The testimony of the last witness...was enough and nothing else is needed to show the character of this transaction from beginning to end. This boy was a long way from the property and he had a right to rely on representations of those who had peculiar knowledge of it. They fooled him and they fooled him to the top of his bent. He is entitled to every dollar he sues for and the return of expenses he incurred in going to view the property at Bayocean. He is entitled to it all.

Judge McGinn told the engineer's attorney that had the attorney asked for $250.00 exemplary damages he would have awarded that also. There is no evidence that T. B. or T. Irving Potter attended this trial. By this time both had left the scene. This was not a lone case.

At the time of McNurlen vs. T. B. Potter Realty Company, another action was beginning to billow steam.

Apparently Frank McNurlen's attorney was in the nick of time with his suit. In another Circuit Court (Judge Gaten), numerous purchasers of lots in Bayocean had joined together asking that a receiver be appointed for the company. Mr. S. B. Vincent of the State of Oregon Corporation Department had already testified before Judge Gaten that the pavement ("driveways") laid in some parts of Bayocean was "of the flimsiest sort and would not stand heavy traffic." Vincent also told the court that "contracts for the lots called for 28 miles of pavement whereas only three and one-half miles had been laid."

Where was Thomas Benton Potter?

In our 1983 book, *Maimed By the Sea*, we wrote:

> ...his wife reported that he became suddenly violently ill
> ...bolted from his home in the middle of the night and was
> never seen again.

Is this just folklore added to many unusual events at Bayocean? Finally, after locating his grandsons, we asked them in 1989. Two said they didn't know, one intimating it could be so. "But I never met my grandfather. I was only 2 when he died. I only heard grownups talking in my early years." The third grandson shrugged it off saying such a remark was "typical" of Potter's wife, "mater" as she was called, who had the ability to think quickly on her feet, the remark plausibly being a retort to someone who brought up the subject.

From a chronological standpoint, T. B. Potter purchased a mansion in Alameda, California, at 1118 San Antonio Avenue about 1912. (This building was torn down in 1970 and the lot sub-divided.) With the failure of his health at Bayocean, it is presumed his wife left with him for Alameda immediately thereafter. Potter died in his Alameda home on April 29, 1916. He was 50. His obituary was carried in the *Oregonian* and in the *Alameda Evening Times-Star* both on May 1. Sometime later, his widow distributed his ashes in San Francisco Bay from a ferry boat. According to the obituary in the Alameda paper, "[His] health began to fail six years ago." Could this "failure" have been a case of too much stress as a result of his extremely aggressive Bayocean promotions?

After both Potters had left Bayocean the resort entered a financial decline from which it would never recover. Undoubtedly part of this decline was brought about by bad publicity from various court actions. Also, there was a general belt-tightening with the start of the First World War. Because both Potters were driving forces and able to influence people to visit Bayocean even with its unfavorable transportation conditions, was it possible their successors were not "self-starters" thus those of the public still interested in property simply looked elsewhere? ☐

Our home at Bayocean. Cottage Park.

Dr. John Potter Dobbins, San Marino, California, grandson of T. B. Potter and son of Potter's daughter, Arleta, displays the only known remaining blanket from the Bayocean Hotel. This blanket is wool. Dr. Dobbins has presented this blanket to the Tillamook Pioneer Museum. (Lower) Many professional groups held conventions at Bayocean, including the Oregon Pharmaceutical Association which met in convention at the hotel in July 1913. Badge presented to the Pioneer Museum by Dr. J. Kenneth Munford, Corvallis, Oregon, whose mother attended.

CHAPTER 5

BAYOCEAN AND
THE U.S. MAIL

One thing that T. B. Potter did not have to contend with was how to get mail on and off the spit. He did a lot of things there, including the building of a town, but credit for the Post Office is not his. Postal service was already old when he first set foot on the spit in 1906. The existing Post Office was called "Barnegat, Oregon," and was located about two miles south of the eventual hotel site. It had been open since April 28, 1891, with A. B. Hallock, Postmaster.* The location is presumed to have been on Webley Hauxhurst property, Hauxhurst having filed for a Donation Land

BARNEGAT. Established Apr. 28, 1891, discontinued Oct. 31, 1895. Re-established Mar. 26, 1898, discontinued Feb. 4, 1909, and moved to Bayocean (town) as BAYOCEAN on Feb. 4, 1909. Operated as 4th Class Post Office until Mar. 31, 1953, being forced to close as the town was nearly abandoned due to breach of the spit. Service re-established on firmer ground as CAPE MEARES Apr. 1, 1953, discontinued Jan. 31, 1954. Since then the residents of the Cape Meares Community receive mail on a rural route out of Tillamook.

---

* Microfilm of *The Tillamook Headlight,* for Dec. 13, 1900, reveals Bargegat post office was moved and operated from the Cape Meares Lighthouse apparently for about eight months. For details refer to *Oregon's Seacoast Lighthouses. See:* Bibliography.

Claim there in 1867. (The northern end, Kincheloe Point, was not filed on until nearly twenty years later.) Potter petitioned the Post Office Department to change the name and to move the Post Office to his town. His request was granted. Effective February 4, 1909, a Thursday, the Post Office became "Bayocean, Oregon."

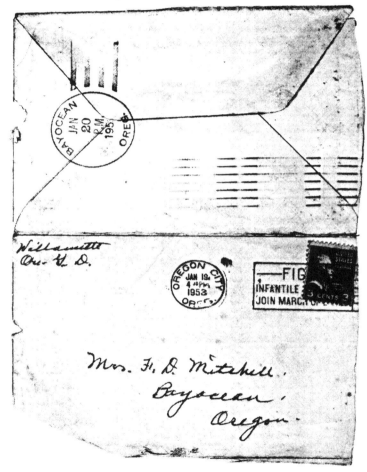

This letter to Mrs. Mitchell, received at the Bayocean Post Office January 20, 1953, is one of the last pieces of mail received. Just about everyone else had moved away. The spit had been broken. Access was now as it had been in Potter's day: by boat only.

Postal historians consider covers (envelopes) bearing a Barnegat postmark as extremely rare. But just because an official announcement gives an official date of change, there are many reasons why these changes are not made on schedule. The 2¢ stamped envelope illustrated here from the Mader Collection, is clearly canceled "BARNEGAT, OR-EG. MAR 23, 1909." This is a month and half *after* the official date of change, possibly still used because the new BAYOCEAN, OREGON device had not yet arrived. Just when the new postmark went into use has not been determined. Mary Jones is reported to have been the first Postmaster. Evelyn Reeder was Postmaster when the office closed.

Records show that Mrs. Mitchell was appointed Postmaster in 1913 and served until her retirement in 1947. Afterward, Mrs. Russell Hoover, Sr., was Postmaster for a short time until she and her husband moved to Tillamook.

Dispatch as well as receipt of mail at Bayocean immediately after the 1948 washout was hectic. Russell Hoover wrote, "It was trying times as my wife was Postmaster and we had many narrow escapes getting across these gaps between waves."

The Bayocean Post Office served over four decades and was a "4th Class Office." After the final washout in November 1952, Mrs. Hoover is reported to have exclaimed, "There is no town left. No people. No business. No more mail...." Thus the government closed the Bayocean Post Office on March 31, 1953. Service resumed at the new CAPE MEARES, OREG. Post Office which opened on safer ground the next day, April 1, 1953. But that Post Office didn't survive postal reorganization favoring individual street numbers in rural areas, so the Office was closed January 31, 1954. Mail for the Cape Meares Community now comes from Tillamook on a motorized route. □

Looking north from base of spit about 1947. White building in center, rear, is Mitchell's store. Car parked across the road is at Jackson Gap, so named as Mr. Jackson had a home nearby. Spit breachings occurred here in 1939, 1942, 1948 and 1952.

CHAPTER 6

FINALLY A ROAD

In the mid-1920s some refinancing became available and the first consideration was to build a road from Tillamook to Bayocean. The road followed the shore of Tillamook Bay to the spit, then turned on to the spit at about 1st Street in the original Cape Meares Community. The road picked up the name "Bay Boulevard" once on the spit, continued along the bay side to the center of town. The major street intersection in town was Bay Blvd. and 12th Avenue. Mitchell's store was on the southwest corner. The Bayside Hotel (owned by Mitchell) was on the southeast

Houses fell into the ocean so frequently that the local press did not report them.

corner. Twelfth Avenue ran a few yards east of Bay Blvd. to the dock which extended into Tillamook Bay. To the west, 12th Avenue went up the dune and was one of the major routes to both the Natatorium and to the Hotel.

(Visitors on the spit today will want to note the locations mentioned. Today's parking lot at the end of the breakwater is approximately 850 yards southeast from the corner of Bay Blvd. and 12th Avenue. Unless the ocean claws it down, there is a remains of a small knoll slightly northwest of the parking lot on the edge of the low dune at the high tide line. For years careful walkers could find a short length of paved "driveway" leading up the little knoll and breaking off at the edge but this is now overgrown (1989). The pavement is all that's left of High Street (see photo page 116). Beyond the edge of the cliff a few more feet, on the ocean side, was Louis Bennett's home. He took it apart board at a time and moved it to his lot in the Cape Meares Community. All he lost was his garage and his wife's daffodils—page 111. (See map page 42.)

There had been three hotels, a grand natatorium, a

dance pavilion and a busy business center. By the time the road arrived, the dance hall was gone. The natatorium was about to go and the largest hotel was all but abandoned. "Mitchell's Corners" had the main activity except for the dock. On the dock were several boat rental firms catering to visiting fishermen. Potter had promised a motion picture theatre but it was never built. But he did install projection equipment in the gallery of the "nat" where there were about 1,000 seats.

When the road to the spit was nearly completed, Mitchell installed a glass-top, gravity-flow gasoline pump in front of his store. He would be ready for business—the only gas pump on the spit. His brand was TEXACO.

☆   ☆   ☆

Once the road became a reality, many who had patronized other resorts along the Tillamook County ocean frontage decided to visit Bayocean. Things became rosier and Mitchell's gas pump was busy.

Newspaper accounts of the time said there were about 850 deeded lots plus the Tent City (Cottage Park). Mitchell rubbed his hands with glee hoping Bayocean would have a comeback. Just as this new vigor began to take hold, the dark days of the Depression stifled just about everything. As with other communities nationwide, property was abandoned and people seemed to disappear. As store owners and Postmaster, the Mitchells stayed on along with a handful of others. Some of the down-and-out were permitted to live in the now-abandoned hotel for free. A few fished for a living.

With the road came two concerns not earlier envisioned. The first was the loss of privacy. In the early years of the resort, if one was not a "Potter guest" the only way to get there was with a row or sailboat or a raft. (Outboard motors had been invented but there were none known in the Pacific Northwest until much later.) Damage by visiting picnickers or by casual fishermen must have been minimal as there is no mention of it. Along with the opening of the road came the "fun" for some fellows who owned Model A

Ford cars. It became a lark to hold races over what was left of the concrete "driveways." As an old-timer told the authors, "You know, as poor as those concrete slabs with their exposed cobbles were at Potter's old resort, those streets were better than many of those in Tillamook!"

The pavement was only so-called residential driveway width except for some wider areas near "Mitchell's Corners" near the dock and 12th Avenue, which was the main route to the hotel and to the natatorium. Although the streets were in weathered condition—some heaved with the years and many broken—they were kept clear of drifting sand because Mitchell would not allow sand to cover the streets and "detract from the beauty of Bayocean."

The other concern was vandalism.

At the hotel, that once-proud honeymoon haven, the grand piano was shoved down a flight of stairs and wrecked. In the pantry where thousands of plates, cups, saucers, glasses and other pieces for table settings were stored, vandals smashed them until the pile on the floor was nearly three feet deep. Of this ware, only one unbroken platter is known. That piece is in the hands of a woman who honeymooned there decades ago and kept it for a souvenir.

Erma Lewis, who loaned this picture, wrote, "... [this] beautiful home found a watery grave. One wouldn't think a hill covered with trees would succumb but it did." Car appears to be 1937 Ford.

Finally a Road

"Mitchell's Corners." With the town nearly abandoned, Potter's "driveways" became raceways for those with cars who wanted to contest, Bayside Hotel (left) at intersection of Bay Blvd. and 12th Street.

This Shanango china platter, from Bayocean Hotel dining room, was a "souvenir" of Vernice Goodman's honeymoon trip to the spit.

The porcelain plate breaks
Fragments splinter everywhere
Preservation lost.
— ©Lillian Baker 1989

Outright theft of goods from Bayocean appears to have been a major concern during the depression then again after the severe washout of 1948. Many people, on being frightened that the sea would claim them as well as their homes, packed what they could carry and pulled out, abandoning the remainder.

Law enforcement was in Tillamook—a long way off. After the grand washout of 1952, anyone who wanted to take a motorboat to the "island" for a visit did and some came back, after dark, with much loot. It almost seems that what was not stolen was broken. □

The most outstanding piece of art to survive the destruction of Bayocean Park, to come to authors' attention, is bust of SAPPHO, 6th Century B.C. Greek poetess. Johan Poulsen imported the figure from Italy. This piece was salvaged from his mansion by Swan Hawkinson before the house fell into the ocean. From the 11th Edition of *Encyclopedia Brittanica* (1910) we learn that SAPPHO was "by no means a paragon of virtue." Hawkinson presented the bust to the Pioneer Museum in Tillamook where it can be seen in the Bayocean Room.

CHAPTER 7

BAYOCEAN'S SCHOOL

The town, Bayocean, Tillamook County, Oregon, was definitely on the map. There was a voting precinct and a public school. In 1932 a teacher, Otta L. Biggs, helped her class of sixteen boys and girls aged five through twelve, plant a tree. The planting was part of Washington's Birthday celebration. Teacher Biggs wrote a note about planting the tree on school grounds then she had each student sign the paper. They put the sheet of tablet paper in a bottle, sealed the bottle then buried it alongside the young tree. Twenty-seven years later the tree was uprooted during a severe storm when breakers crashed against the land again. The tree, when planted in the school yard, had been about three-quarters of a mile from the ocean. Now it was on the beach.

Delores Snyder of Cape Meares was beachcombing when she noticed a broken bottle and stepped forward to investigate. She found a note in the bottle's remains. The paper was a little tattered but was still legible.

Bayocean, Oregon
February 19, 1932

We the undersigned, did plant this alder tree on the Bayocean school grounds on the above date in memory of the 200th anniversary of Washington's birth. Pupils of the Bayocean School:

1.	Jens Pederson 5	9.	Molly Maryalice Varnum 10
2.	Arthus Solverson 6	10.	Louise Clairette Campbell 9
3.	(torn paper) Campbell 7	11.	Bettiana Watkins 9
4.	Verena Watkins 6	12.	Delores Biggs (paper torn) [9]
5.	Evelyn Pederson 8	13.	Frances House 12
6.	Olive Jean Hays 8	14.	John Edward Hays 12
7.	Barbara Jean House 8	15.	Robert H. Watkins 12
8.	Jansina Nevada Pederson 9	16.	John L. Allen 12

Otta L. Biggs, teacher

65

Only one of the original signers still lives in the area: Bob Watkins. Delores Snyder presented the note to him. the newspapers made quite a story about it. Bob remarked on learning about it, "As I remember, we were supposed to plant an apple tree. But 1932 was a pretty tough year and we couldn't find an apple tree so we planted an alder."

The school building was not lost to the sea, for folks got together and moved it to where it rests today in the 5600 block of 4th Street NW at Cape Meares Community. In 1989 the building still serves as the Community Hall. Lou Bennett kept repair parts for the water system in a closet. Until his death, Bennett lived next door.

As we have seen, Potter did not include a fire department in the plans for his town and neither did he provide a church. But after the school was built visiting clergy and traveling "missionaries" held services there. The school was equipped with a piano, and missionary helpers from Tillamook donated hymnbooks.

Mrs. Alton (Jean Randall) Hopkins, now living in Southern Oregon, is the daughter of Barney and Mrs. Randall. She told the authors she and her sister Hazel attended summer Bible School and worship services in the building while it was still at Bayocean. A Mr. and Mrs. Baker were the leaders at that time. With little else to do, many of the year-around residents attended whatever functions were held at the school, be the activities religious

Louis L. Bennet, in charge of Cape Meares Water District in 1970s with old hymn books in hand, stands in doorway of Bayocean School now on 4th St. N.W. Cape Meares Community.

Bayocean Bible School, 1940, was directed by Rev. and Mrs. Baker, and met in the schoolhouse. Back row, left to right: Mrs. Baker, Opal Williams, May Lou Ried, Shirley Sherwood, Hazel Randall, Theo DeVries, Kenny DeVries, Jean Randall, Dorothy Hlippert, Maude Andrews, Mr. Baker, Bobby Ried, Howard Sherwood. Front row, left to right: Betty Flippert, Darrow Flippert, Carol Sherwood, Ruth DeVries, Mary Baker, Jean DeVries, Betty Ann Coats, Martha Baker, Cynthia Coats, and two Webb boys, first name of one was Kelly, other not recalled.

It appears that religious services were very basic, non-denominational in nature, and if nothing else brought the residents together to a common thought. During another season, Bonnie White and June Pearson came from Tillamook to lead the services.

While interviewing Mr. Bennett inside the old school, he dug around and produced three hymnals which had been left there and were moved along with the building. These are *Fellowship Hymns*, 1910 edition, published by the Y.M.C.A.; *Hymns of Praise Numbers One and Two Combined*, 1941 edition, Hope Publishing Company; and *Tabernacle Hymns No. 3* (no date as the title page is missing). The names of Bonnie White and June Pearson, and "Tillamook, Oregon" are written in purple ink inside the front cover. Bennett gave the books to the authors who, in 1989, presented them to the museum.

After the building was set up as the Community Hall at Cape Meares, visiting clergy came for a short time. In recent years the hall serves as the voting place for the Water District and in summer is the site of the weekly community-wide pot-luck dinners. □

(Top to bottom) "Portable" track was moved about the spit to construction sites as needed. When not hauling building materials and supplies, Dinky engine pulled flat cars of people for "joy riding." Was the overload of people just to pose for this picture? Rare closeup of Vulcan engine.

CHAPTER 8

POTTER'S RAILROAD

We learned from advertising blurbs that T. B. Potter had a "dinky" railroad on the spit primarily for use in construction. We also learned the entire rail operation was highly "portable" as his construction crews moved the tracks as needed. But what could be found today to validate that a railroad had indeed existed at Bayocean? Literally, we had to "dig" it out!

"Buck" Sherwood's family is one of several families who have lived in the Cape Meares area for years. We talked with him and with others. Buck recalled noticing what he described as a set of very narrow gauge tracks embedded in the road near the south end of the spit. He remembered these tracks had been cut off on each side of the road. He said he never paid much attention to the tracks but he did remember seeing them before the 1952 washout.

After viewing one of Potter's handbills where he advertised "A 'Joy Ride' On The Bayocean Railroad," and now being in possession of one of his early brochures showing tracks embedded in the pavement of Twelfth Avenue, we organized a comprehensive search. (See page 48.)

In the spring of 1972, a team was called together to beachcomb the spit hoping to find some trace of the "dinky" railroad. (Visitors will note the old rails used as a fence at the present parking area on the spit, but these rails are the wrong size.) The search started at low tide along the flat beach. By noon we located the remains of Hicks' well which was the main checkpoint on our map. Even at this low water, the well casing was still quite a distance out. Just a little north of the casing the team leader found a metal object at water's edge. It was dark and long. The end was firmly stuck in the sand. The tide had turned and young waves were beginning to lap at our feet. We had no time to

Dale Webber (left) member of team searching for evidence of Potter's railroad, steadies beach-combed rail found during very low tide. Bert (right) in act of pulling rail from gravel beach. (Inset) Door-stopper size length of rail—24 inches—also found same day classed by rail-roaders as "21-pound rail" intended for light service.

lose. We bent over the object then wrenched at it in elbow-deep, clear, cold sea water. It took two of us to pull it loose. We immediately identified it as a length of light-weight rail. The rail was rusty from years of being washed by the sea and being bleached by hot summer sun at low tide. The rail was badly sprung. It was about twenty feet long. We hauled it farther up the beach away from the approaching tide and looked it over closely. Next we photographed it. Still later we moved it off the beach to a "hiding place."

Upon this rail the Bayocean "Dinky" Vulcan engine

had once hauled building materials for a great resort and was used for "joy riding" visitors on happy weekends.

On another inspection of the area, we beachcombed a piece of rusty rail only 24 inches long.

Wouldn't it be great if all beachcombing could be as fruitful? ☐

Bert Webber and Gene Elliott beachcombed this hot water tank at Bayocean in 1983. Piece of Potter driveway in foreground.

CHAPTER 9

A MATTER OF JETTIES

For years the people of Tillamook City, Bay City and surrounding area, had asked the U.S. Army Corps of Engineers to improve the harbor. Finally, in the years 1914-1917 the Engineers built a 5,400-foot long jetty on the north side of the entrance to Tillamook Bay. Many old-timers declared this jetty, with no matching jetty on the south, was the cause of the erosion to the spit and eventual destruction of the town of Bayocean. While these folks agreed they had no scientific evidence, they would talk about this anywhere they could get an audience. Some of these folks claimed to have invested in building lots at Bayocean, the lots washed into the sea and they were certain the Corps of Engineers had caused what they called the "Bayocean problem."

With the advantages of decades of study by an assortment of official agencies, the cause of the loss of sand along the Tillamook Spit sea front has finally been established. First, let's investigate what happened in years past.

Studies of the Tillamook Bay and Bar entrance, with improvements in mind, date back to 1888. A survey in 1897 was followed by another in 1902. These investigations resulted in some in-bay diking and dredging. The first mention of constructing a "jetty entrance" to the bay appears in 1907. A resurvey in 1909 restudied the 1902 and 1907 work and sought to determine if conditions had changed. In a report from the United States Engineer Office of October 1910, Colonel John Biddle wrote: "This bay and bar have been repeatedly examined with a view of improvement. The communities [Tillamook City and Bay City] have now made definite offers to contribute toward a deep-water project."

The involvement between the Federal Government and

the two cities is documented in *House Document No. 349* of the 62nd Congress, 2d Session (December 21, 1911). The paper outlines what harbor improvements the cities desired, what were recommended and how local participation in the costs would be handled. The negotiations took a long time. To summarize, the work wanted by the local interests was in two parts. [1.] They wanted a twenty-foot deep channel through the ocean bar, and [2.] They sought some dredging to certain depths in specified places within the bay.

The Corps of Engineers answered that the request for a deep harbor entrance "would involve construction of two jetties at the entrance of the bay. Improvement was recommended on the condition that twenty-five percent of the costs be contributed by the local interests." The total project was valued at slightly over $2,200,000. After certain other obligations were included, the Federal government would be responsible for about $1,300,000.

The Board of Engineers for Rivers and Harbors reviewed the proposed projects and the funding plan as required by law. The Board could not agree that resulting benefits would justify the cost. The Corps reported back to the people of the two localities and soon received a reply from the cities involved, which the Corps transmitted to the Board of Rivers and Harbors: "The communities found themselves unable or unwilling to contribute to the improvement proposed." This was on March 10, 1910. The proposed project was "held in abeyance pending possible future action on the part of the localities."

The use of the bay by ocean-going ships had always been minimal because of very limited commerce on the bay. Since the railroad from Portland had been completed in 1911, the main export of local products ($550,000 in cheese in 1909) and prime logs would henceforth go by rail. The only suggested commercial use of the port was for shipping low grade timber by water.

In June 1911, another proposition was sent to the Corps by the cities for "partial execution of the improvement desired." The cities agreed to pay half the costs. What the cities wanted now was for the Corps of Engineers to do

LETTER TO THE PRESIDENT OF THE PORT OF TILLAMOOK.

Tillamook, Oreg., May 11, 1911.

Dear Sir: In the matter of the improvement of Tillamook Bay and Bar, the port of Tillamook, at a meeting of its commissioners held on this date, authorized me to write to you stating that the port of Tillamook is willing to contribute toward the cost of the construction of a north jetty at the mouth of Tillamook Bay for the purpose of deepening the water upon the bar, and of dredging the channel from the mouth of the bay to Bay City to a depth of 16 feet.

As reported to us it is estimated that the cost of this north jetty and of dredging contemplated will amount to approximately $814,000. The port of Bay City, which is interested in the project, has agreed to contribute $200,-000 for this purpose, and the port of Tillamook hereby is expressing its willingness and readiness to contribute to this project a sum sufficient, when added to the contribution offered by the port of Bay City, to equal one-half of the entire cost of the project, the total cost of which is not to exceed $814,000.

Believing that the conditions and prospective commerce to be added by the improvement of the Tillamook Bay and Bar will justify the United States Government in contributing the other half of the cost of this project, and trusting that the same may meet with your approval, I am,

Very respectfully   H. T. Botts
                                         President of the Port of Tillamook

Hon. J. M. Dickinson,
        Secretary of War.

Letter from Port of Tillamook as shown on page 18, *House Document No. 349,* **62nd Congress, 2d Session, December 21, 1911, entitled, "Tillamook Bay and Bar, Oregon."**

---

half the job the Corps specified was needed for effectiveness. In other words, some in-bay dredging plus *only one jetty.* (Italic added.) This, for $814,000. This half-a-job was proposed by the Commissioners of the Port of Tillamook in a letter to the Corps of Engineers dated May 11, 1911. A second letter dated December 8, 1911, from the Port of Bay City, sought improvements "under a project providing for either a north jetty or north and south jetties...giving consent to the United States Engineers for building the north jetty only, if they think it advisable, instead of both north and south jetties, as first contemplated by the Department."

A Matter of Jetties

Potter was well aware of the plans afoot to improve the harbor entrance. His yacht used the waters regularly and such improvement, "will result in the co-operation of the War Department to make this one of the safest of deep water harbors between San Francisco and the Columbia River...a mecca for all tourists." (*The Surf*, January 1, 1912, page 1.) He asserted his influence with the Bayocean Commercial Club which called for an election concerning the formation of the Bayocean Port District. There were 89 votes in the election of October 26, 1911. The measure passed. No records have been found where the Bayocean Port District participated in any of the negotiations with the Corps of Engineers over the matter of the jetties.

In the December 1911 issue of *The Surf* is a page-2 story here reproduced from the original, which quotes the paper in Tillamook:

> Representative Humphreys, of the Rivers and Harbors Committee, will visit Tillamook in a few days. In the meantime, let the Ports of Tillamook, Bay City and Bayocean get together and agree on some course of action. Bayocean, we understand, is ready to make a start on the south jetty, and Tillamook has been advised not to put money into a north jetty. What does the Port of Bay City want?—*Tillamook Headlight.*

Potter's interest in harbor improvement meant more tourists and prospective buyers of his property—nothing else. And he wanted the Army to pay for it.

To the Commissioners of the two towns, the Army Engineers responded, reminding these officials of the "fine shifting gray sand" at the crest of the bar and called to their attention that "tidal currents in the entrance gorge are strong on account of the narrowness (750 feet) and the considerable discharge."

The Army would not guarantee any results with a single jetty and was steadfast in its opinion that the action of a single jetty protruding into the ocean could not be foretold. The Corps pointed out their general experience along the Northwest Coast was that two jetties were needed as good results had not been obtained with a single one. To back their statements, they pointed to second jetties then authorized or begun at Grays Harbor, Washington, and at the mouth of the Columbia River.

The Division Engineer wrote this conclusion:

> It is thought that the jetty proposed will only give temporary relief. While construction is recommended largely on account of the contributions of the parties interested, it is considered that the construction of a second jetty must follow, if satisfactory permanent results are to be obtained.

☆   ☆   ☆

And so the north jetty was built. It was completed in 1917. Between 1920 and 1925, Bayocean residents noticed their broad beach was disappearing. Parts of the peninsula

The ocean crashed through the neck of the spit on January 5, 1939 during high tides and winds. The break severed the water pipe, seen dangling on left, turned Bayocean into an island. With a change in weather, the break partially, temporarily, healed.

(Top to bottom) Rock Crusher Gap 1948. Sea water pours through breached spit into Tillamook Bay. (Center) View toward ocean through gap. Water main in foreground. (Bottom) Looking south at washed out Bay Blvd.

Jackson Gap looking north following 1939 breaching.

fell into the sea. Sand was shifting during winter storms and
some "front yards" were being lost at an alarming rate.
Many of the dwellings were mere summer cabins. These
could be moved easily and some were. In at least one
instance, a distant owner arrived on the spit to spend the
summer but he couldn't find his house. It had fallen into the
sea!

The erosion became worse after the north jetty was
repaired and extended in 1933.

Dr. Samuel N. Dicken, of the Geography Department
of the University of Oregon, pointed out that "soundings
made after the construction of the jetty revealed a loss of
sand from the submerged portion of the beach within the
ten fathom line. Furthermore," he continues, "in similar
situations in various parts of the world, the construction of
jetties or breakwaters has led to erosion of the adjacent
beaches."

In 1948, during a wild winter storm, the sea rushed in
and broke the spit.

As part of the publicity for calling attention to the
problems of washouts, a fisherman, George Blanchard,
brought his twenty-seven-foot oversize gill net boat in
through the gap to emphasize the size of the washout. On

January 2, 1949, the *Sunday Oregonian* reported: "Waves surged through this opening carrying salmon from the sea into the bay in six feet of water."

By this time over twenty homes had fallen into the sea and several hundred feet of frontage had been lost.

We have mentioned frontage losses but some may be concerned how these measurements were taken. Dr. Dicken prepared a report for the Office of Naval Research. His evidence was on a piece of property at Bayocean on an elevation of about fifty feet. The owner had driven a series of stakes in his yard and observed an average rate of erosion of about one foot a year between 1926 and 1932. But erosion occurs in differing amounts depending on the time of year, winter being the heaviest, and erosion may vary from year to year. The stake line measurements during 1932 and 1933 were of such severity that the overall average of land loss rose to six feet a year. Measurements taken from interpretation of aerial photographs between 1939 and 1944 establish an erosion rate of about sixteen feet per year. From 1939 to the date of Dicken's paper in 1960, he reported the erosion in the twenty-one years as averaging about *fifty feet per year*. In the area closer to Cape Meares, where several streets paralleling the ocean were lost one block after another, Dicken reported a loss rate of approximately *twenty-three feet per year* in the same period.

During a season of constant high tides and ferociously high winds in November 1952, the wild breakers broke the spit. This once peninsula became an island.

Big waves had washed over the peninsula several times earlier. The major washouts were: Jackson Gap 1939, 1942, 1948, 1952. Rock Crusher Gap 1948. Natatorium Gap 1939, 1954. One source claims Mitchell's store had "a foot of water and sand in it" after the 1939 wave swept through Natatorium Gap, roared down 11th and 12th Avenues and into the bay!

The title, "Main Gap" seems to have been adopted in 1948 just after the first major partition of the spit.

When the Main Gap washed out on December 5, 1948, the water main was broken. After the breakthrough, Barney

Roaring in on a wild storm, crashing breakers broke the spit on November 13, 1952. At high tide, breach was about one mile wide. Within one month the population of Bayocean dwindled to 6 persons including Mr. and Mrs. F. D. Mitchell.

Randall and Russell Hoover drove to Tillamook to seek help, as drinking water had to be restored to the town as quickly as possible. The power company sent a pole-line construction crew and truck. The men planted a pole at each side of the break then ran a steel cable between the poles. The Tillamook Fire Department loaned 800 feet of fire hose which was stretched across the gap then hoisted and lashed to the cable. It took all day and part of the night to restore the water service.

After the 1952 grand washout, all that remained was Kincheloe Point and as far south as Bayocean townsite. People had become alarmed of the risk, so a few buildings had been removed from the spit just before the big storm.

Quite a number of people never built anything on their lots and some lots were claimed by the County for failure to pay taxes, but this didn't matter now. Many of these lots

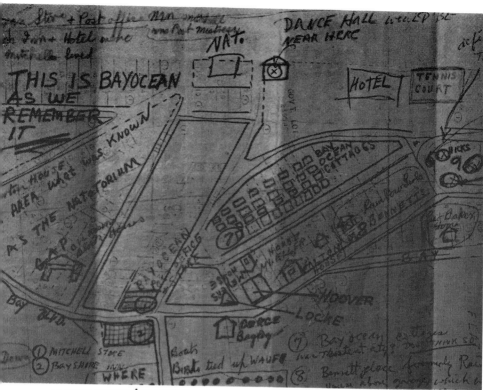

were now under water.

The break was about as wide as San Francisco's Golden Gate—one mile. Over 1,000 acres of choice oyster beds, established in Tillamook Bay in 1928, were covered with fine sand within minutes and lost forever.

The ocean was indeed on the rampage! The road which had been sought for so long was now under water around the clock. Access to Bayocean was now as it had been in Potter's earliest time: by boat only. In addition, the tidal surge caused waves in the bay which lapped sea water over the levies onto adjoining farmland. People living in the east bayside communities were suddenly scared, as "the Bayocean problem" now became, they thought, a direct threat to them.

What little commerce there had been over the Tilla-mook bar ground to a stop. The log and lumber tonnage across the bar dropped from 84,000 short tons just before the breakthrough, to only 7,000 in two years. The next year the Corps of Engineers reported "zero" tonnage.

There was a general revision of maps in 1954 so cartographers illustrated Bayocean as an island.

People decried the loss of the peninsula and many blamed the Corps of Engineers for building only one jetty. The Corps kept silent, but looked into the records and clearly saw their recommendations of forty years earlier for two jetties and saw that the people demanded only one be built. Most of the present complainers had not been born when the earlier negotiations had occurred and those older folk still around chose not to remember. But the cry was unanimous and directed squarely at the Corps: "You fix that peninsula!"

The Corps seems to have been on the defensive in some of its statements, probably reacting to public pressure.

The Corps stated their long-standing policy that the Federal Government had no legal interests in the problem, that the Corps participated in harbor development and maintenance—not in rebuilding sand dunes for people's front yards, roads of access, or for the benefit of oyster farmers. □

The once busiest corner in town, 12th Avenue and Bay Blvd., abandoned after the breaching of 1952. Mitchell Bldg. at left. Note capped gasoline pipes to Mitchell's underground 550-gallon tank near curb where he once had a Texaco gasoline pump.

CHAPTER 10

THE CAUSE

Scientists in the Sea Grant Program at Oregon State University issued a statement in the mid-1970s on the cause of the erosion at Bayocean that washed out the spit. Stated here in non-technical language, they wrote that the loss of the peninsula was caused by the construction of a single jetty on the north side of the bay entrance in 1914-1917, and accelerated by the rebuilding and extension of that single jetty in 1932-1933.

We recall the Corps of Engineers told the cities of Tillamook and Bay City that a single jetty would not work, but the people of those two towns insisted that they only wanted one jetty—(half-a-job)—so that's what the Corps built.

The technical study found that erosion started about 1920 and became pronounced in the mid-1930s during the building of the extension of the single jetty. The scientists pointed out all of the changes in the shoreline resulted from local rearrangements of the beach due to the "disturbed equilibrium" following jetty construction.

As the ocean picked up sand from the spit, it deposited it primarily in two places. The first was behind (north of) the new single jetty and the second place was in the channel of the by entrance thus forcing the channel to move north against the new jetty where it created a shoal, or outer bar (ebb-tide delta), at harbor entrance. This shoal reduced the water depth and became a hazard for boats trying to enter the channel even in moderate conditions.

That the lengthening of the single jetty in the early 1930s had a specific impact on the equilibrium of the beach is evident when we observe there were a series of washouts afterward but none earlier. While the jetty extension was in progress, the first "attack" on the natatorium occurred

83

The natatorium opened in 1912. By 1932 the ocean had undermined the concrete sidewalk and front of the building causing the walls to sag so the roof collaspsed. Some of the lumber was salvaged and used in the construction of the Sherwood home on 4th Street in Cape Meares Community. What was left of the "nat" went down during the 1939 winter storms. At extremely low tide some of the very large concrete corner blocks, as well as the concrete septic tank (shown) can be seen in the mid-1980s. This photograph was taken about 1940.

The North Jetty.

The Cause

Looking north from base of spit right after breaching in November 1952. Compare with picture on page 59. Note snapped off power-telephone pole in wash area and downed lines. With each succeeding high tide, neck of the spit was totally reduced. When maps were redrawn in 1954, Bayocean was shown as an island, as only Kincheloe Point remained.

with the undermining of the sidewalk in front of the building in 1932. The building's foundations were dislodged by 1936 so the roof fell in. In 1939 the sea ripped through what became known as the "Natatorium Gap," destroying what was left of the building, and sent water rushing down Bayocean's streets and into the bay as earlier related. By the 1940s there was no trace of the natatorium other than a few chunks of concrete strewn about the beach. □

CHAPTER 11

OUR SUMMERS AND
MR. MITCHELL

Greta Forbish, with her husband and then young family, spent many summers vacationing at resorts in Tillamook County. She said that some of the most amazing and memorable trips were to Bayocean. Her recollections are warm and exciting and are contained in a series of letters to the authors. Many of her experiences at Bayocean form the basis of this chapter.

Although we hadn't planned it that way, our acquaintance with Bayocean began in 1939. We owned a $150 used 1931 Cadillac limousine which we loaded for a holiday at the beach. Our home was in Portland so preparations for a long weekend trip had to be carefully made. There were the children, Grandma and the dog, plus all the usual family paraphernalia one hauls along on such an excursion. Never having been able to afford a vacation before, we took the advice of a friend and wrote a couple of days in advance to reserve a cabin at Netarts. When we arrived, the manager uttered a genial welcome but assured us that everything had been booked for a month previously. We were stunned. The manager suggested we try Bayocean, smiling at us and assuring "there is probably plenty of accommodation there— ha, ha, ha!" So we went back along the narrow, twisting, graveled lane past Oceanside, then zig-zagged some more until we reached a junction—there wasn't any sign—which took us almost to the ocean's edge then a sharp turn to the north and out along a spit.

Bayocean wasn't impressive. The rutted road along the spit led us past the aroma of *Eau de Mudflattes* until we reached the old original Bayside Hotel. The disintegrating

two-story building was across the street from the former
general store and its second-floor apartments, both by now
long vacant. We were met by an exuberant committee of
one—Francis Drake Mitchell—a sprightly gnome who
rubbed his hands gleefully as he directed us to a parking
spot. He was delighted over the resurgence of activity in his
beloved homeland. Several other cars were parked, indicat-
ing to us that others had also accepted this haven in
desperation.

Francis Drake Mitchell *was* Bayocean. An apple-
cheeked little man, he bounced with enthusiasm for his
Paradise and scampered rather than walked. He was a
torrent of information! In contrast, his dark, heavy, placid
wife seemed like an immovable rock about which a sprightly
lizard scuttled.

"Now, Mr. Mitchell," she would chide him tolerantly,
"You don't know that for sure. You might be exaggerat-
ing."

"But, Mrs. Mitchell," he would protest, "you know
I'm right!"

"You may be right," she would respond amiably, "but

Looking east down 12th Avenue to Bay Hotel—Mitchell Building on right at corner. Photo probably made just after breaching of spit and abandonment as Corps of Engineers made plans to raze the town. (Lower) Bay Hotel on left, Mitchell Building at right, view faces south.

it doesn't do to say so until you're sure of your facts, Mr. Mitchell.''

That was one of the endearing things about them—the old fashioned courtesy they showed to one another. It may have started as a loving jest when they were first married but became a habit. We never heard them address each other except as "Mr." and "Mrs."

Before unpacking, my husband and I alighted from our car to look around. There was no question about it. The hotel was dismal and dilapidated. We were assigned two bedrooms overlooking the mud flats. Our host assured us that the tide would eventually come in, giving us a beautiful view. The mattresses were damp and musty and Mrs. Mitchell, whom we had also just met, had preceded us and was serenely running an old-fashioned warming pan over their surfaces causing steam to rise. Fortunately we had our own blankets!

It was growing dark. With Mr. Mitchell as guide, we went across the street and invaded his old store with flashlight in search of sustenance. But it was of little satisfaction for the stock in his erstwhile establishment had diminished to a few dusty cans of beans and corned beef and—shades of glory—a couple of jars of almond-stuffed onions and caviar! We also noticed some dubious, damp packages of breakfast food and potato chips which bent lifelessly at the pressure of one's fingers. Observing that we were obviously in need of a larger variety of foods than we could find here, Mr. Mitchell made the rounds of his guests to inquire of their nutritional desires, then he tore off to Tillamook to fulfill them.

It was awhile but Mitchell returned with the required groceries. There were bakery goods, milk, coffee, onions, cheese, bread, soda pop and many other things as requested. Quickly, after he finished his meticulous accounting for every penny, he brought us all together, then flung open the doors to the vast kitchen which, he announced, was for all of us to use. That kitchen had the biggest sink I've ever seen, two capacious wood-burning ranges stoked to white heat, a plethora of sizable pots, kettles and pans—remnants of the former majesty of the kitchen service. (Ever try to heat a single can of chili in a 2-gallon kettle?)

We females fluttered about and courteously backed away from each other for a few minutes but presently began to chatter and share the accommodations as well as what had brought us to this strange and desolate spot—all of them duplications of our own experience: "Try Bayocean, there is probably plenty of accommodation there—ha, ha, ha!"

Reproduced from original cartoons courtesy of Greta Forbish

Presently we were sharing foodstuffs and pans.

"Oh, I brought along a can of cinnamon. Just a minute, I'll find it."

"Would you like to put your loaf of garlic bread at the other end of my pan of biscuits?"

"My kids are just crazy about hot dogs. Would you swap a couple of hamburger patties?"

Eventually we fed our families at the half dozen big tables after the kids had investigated the bay and trekked up the broken street that led to the top of the dunes.

After dinner Mr. Mitchell, quivering with delight, led us into the parlor in which there was a large wood stove radiating heat that almost took the curse off the mildewed rump-sprung furnishings. The night had turned chilly. By now there were eight or nine children and a dozen or so adults. One lady managed to pump some notes out of a wheezy old reed organ and another consented, without any

90

BREE & LARRY WENT CLAMMING IN
THE BAY YESTERDAY - 5 A.M.

SEQUEL: CHOWDER

pressure, to oblige with some "vocal renditions." But her renderings sent many of us out into the chilly, damp night to walk off our suppers until it was safe to come in again!

The next morning was clear, warm and sparkling bright. A few guests left, but were soon replaced by others. In mid-morning, our family trudged up "Cardiac Hill," as I dubbed it, then down its ocean side to the site of the once-great natatorium. Chunks of concrete and some twisted metal half buried in the sand were still being washed by the incoming tide. Laden with blankets, sweaters, suntan potions, wieners, potato chips, marshmallows and cartons of "imitation" grape and "artificial" orange drinks (and considerably hampered by our dachshund who had to be carried over the soft sand), we sauntered the three-mile trip along the coast, headed for the north end of the spit. It was with dismay that we observed the once-grand hotel—in earlier years a place in great demand by honeymooners, trembling precariously at the edge of a cliff over one hundred feet above the beach. One corner had already crashed to the beach below. Other than that, the outlook was magnificent. The sea and sandy beach were on the left. A densely wooded area was above and on the right.

When we reached the end of the spit, we gathered small driftwood and built a huge bonfire. As the fire died, we braced ourselves against the wind-swept smoke holding wieners on sticks. Soon we were insulting our interiors with partly-raw, partly-scorched frankfurters followed by charred marshmallows. We spread our blankets then we adults alternately dozed and raised up to check the kids who scampered in and out of the surf.

As sunset approached we plodded our way back, ravenous and thirsty. We were beginning to be uncomfortable from sunburn which had ignored our lotions.

While dinner of cheese sandwiches, grilled on the massive stove, and canned spaghetti was underway, we found ourselves trapped in the kitchen where Mr. Mitchell benevolently harangued us from the doorway on the benefits to be acquired from the purchase of certain lots. He envisioned a future that would make past glories look small. We listened as well as our drooping eyelids and our now genuinely bothersome sunburns would permit, then thanked him for the information. As our total funds were less than $50, we were forced to ignore the bonanza without discussion. We retired immediately afterward into our creaky beds. If the gelatin soprano obliged again with "Would God I Were A Tender Apple Blossom," or, "Share A Pot With Gypsy John," we never knew it. As far as we were concerned, the pot we were sharing was quite far down the hall. It couched somnolently in one corner of the cavernous bathroom in the company of its ceiling-high, pull-chain flush tank. Neither Gypsy John nor Tender Apple Blossom was welcome!

The next morning, Sunday, was another bright day. We spent the morning, after hot cakes and steaming syrup, hiking along forest paths on Kincheloe Point. But we had a

long drive ahead of us so we packed up and left by noon.

Mr. Mitchell held us with his mesmeric eyes and insisted, "I hope you will all come back."

"We will, we will," we chorused.

As a matter of fact, he was convinced everybody would return once they had explored the delights of Bayocean for they would realize its great potential.

We did come back. Many times. But the next decade lapses into a gentle blur of progressive deterioration. The old Bay Hotel, which had been one of the first buildings constructed, never again received guests.

On later trips we made our vacation headquarters at Cottage park. This area was about one block west, toward the center of the spit. More properly, we stayed at **COT AGE PA K** as it was proclaimed in two-foot high wooden letters swinging from a chain. The last time we were there, winter storms had further reduced the sign to just **OT AG AK** as the letters dropped from their rusty chain and were never replaced.

There were many cottages, really cabins built on the former wood platforms from the earlier "tent city." But I never counted or investigated them further than the

These cabins became post office, convenience grocery and office for rentals in Cottage Park after 1947. All area shown was eventually claimed by the sea.

woodshed. Each cabin was about the size of a railroad caboose which had been set end-to-end duplicating one another in reverse. A minuscule dining room-living room-kitchen with a sink and a wood range, a table, four straight chairs and a rocking chair made up the furnishings in the "front" room. The rocker banged into one's ankles no matter where one tried to move it. There was a flimsy partition and a burlap curtain for the bedroom which was just large enough for two double beds. Through the narrow aisle one could slide to the rear where a small closet contained a bureau with immovable drawers and a toilet. This was an extremely companionable arrangement for you were separated from the people in back only by a large tin Bull Durham sign which had been tacked up to reinforce the weakening partition between the two units.

Refrigeration was provided in the form of a screened orange crate which was nailed on the outside of the cottage near the door. This "cooler" was quite adequate for milk, fruits and butter. Although Chambers of Commerce talk about warm, sunny summers, which we did have frequently at Bayocean, there seemed nearly always to be some rain,

FOR SALE

I am forced to sell some of my choicest lots in Bayocean at a sacrifice.

The Tillamook-Bayocean Co. has made false statements to the citizens of Bayocean and the community at large, stating the natatorium would be open for business this season. They have failed to make their word good and have placed some of us in an embarrassing position financially, this situation must be met at once.

I borrowed $500.00 from the Tillamook National Bank to finance my store and this money must be paid back when due if my credit is to remain good. My goods are on the shelf and very few customers to buy, certainly some one is looking for a bargain.

Your choice of any lot at one-half of what we paid for them in 1907.

F. D. Mitchell   Ba

F. D. Mitchell had these posters printed in the spring of 1914 as evidence indicates it was at that time serious squabbles began between Potter, Mitchell, and others. A single copy of this poster was discovered in a second-hand store in 1972 by the authors, which was used for this illustration. The Mitchells (right) in 1947.

"mist" or just fog to keep things cool and the grass green.

A Mr. Hoover, a fine host, was in charge of the cottages in those days and was followed by a Mr. Locke. We tried to schedule our vacations to coincide with minus tides, and our host obligingly rose around 5 a.m. to show us how to rake for crabs. He also told us where to look for peanut-size oysters over near Cape Meares. These midget oysters had to be chipped out of their nests in the rocks with a hammer and pick. They tasted like a combination of clam and oyster and I never heard of them anywhere else. We were also shown where to find cockerels, which seem to become helpless on the mud flats or are buried just beneath the surface. Nothing better than cockerels for chowder, or ground and made into patties then fried.

During the war years some of the cabins were permanently occupied by employees of industries near the city of Tillamook. These folks, mostly men, lived in the rear of the park and regarded us vacationers with deep suspicion, except for one very dedicated gent who spent most of his off-time surf-casting. He was amused at our amateurish attempts and several times he left strings of fresh ocean perch for us, declaring, "God, how I hate sea food!"

During the years we came to know the Mitchells quite well. He loved us because we were the only ones of the original group to return. With the advantages of hind sight, it's a shame we didn't pay more attention to the tales he told. He was a pharmacist when he arrived in 1907 and was eager to open a drug store and establish himself in a growing community. Mr. Mitchell built the first hotel (the one we stayed in), established the first store, appointed himself a one-man Chamber of Commerce to further what he saw as a spectacular future in what was then to be known as "The Millionaires' Playground." Mitchell fought valiantly for every advantage, bubbled with enthusiasm when each new structure went up and the public bought building sites. He was a "possibility thinker" yet according to his own report, was thwarted at every turn by what he called "political chicanery." He was in and out of court like a yo-yo on a string. Although the collapse of the natatorium was a catastrophic blow to him, he did not allow even that event to get him down. He redoubled his efforts to have a breakwater built to prevent further erosion.

So great was Mitchell's obsession, so tireless his ingenuity at prodding and pounding, that in his zeal to further Bayocean he often trod on too many toes. He shyly, but not without pride, showed us sheafs of threatening letters and scurrilous anonymous notes, some couched in the most obscene language. "I'm getting under their skin," he chortled. "They'll have to do something pretty quick!"

During all the summers we vacationed at Bayocean, we never conducted any business in the Post Office, which was in the back of Mitchell's store. Mrs. Mitchell was the Postmaster but Mr. Mitchell handled most of the mail. When we were there, our mail was obligingly delivered in person and whenever we approached with a letter or postal card in hand, Mr. Mitchell would pop out to receive it. He was overjoyed with the cartoons I drew on penny postal

Mitchell's Bayside Hotel as it appeared when Greta Forbish vacationed there probably in 1939. See page 86.

"...we never conducted any business in the Post Office."

cards. He pranced with glee at them and frequently buttonholed passers-by to share the jest and exhibited extreme disappointment when we sent a mere typewritten message. Their Post Office had the usual appointments: dozens of little lock boxes, some of which had the doors missing; the traditional service window with its iron bars, a small counter on which one could write out an "Application for Domestic Money Order" with the infamous Post Office dip pens whose nibs must surely have been used on a dart board, for they never—well, almost never—would write! Also, the usual file of "WANTED" posters from the F.B.I. were displayed, held to the finger-smudged bulletin board with a single straight pin. Why one who was "WANTED" would even conceive of hiding out at Bayocean we could never imagine! There was no light fixture near the Post Office window; but within the official inner-sanctum there was a single cord dangling from the ceiling which contained a near-antique, clear glass, low wattage light globe, screwed into a porcelain socket.

On the beach, the deterioration became more evident with each passing year. The coastline was changing. Winter storm tides crept further up on the land. We beachcombed on every trip and never went back to our cottage empty-handed. Once we found a mass of agates larger than a man's clenched fist. We collected a quantity of them but, finding them too heavy to carry very far, we made a *cache* beneath a stump then left a brightly colored neck scarf on a snag as a marker. When we returned later, we discovered that someone had found our treasure and made off with all the agates as well as the scarf. Our attitude was, "Oh well, we'll get more tomorrow!" But the next days were squally so we spent the time in the cottage. We played "Uncle Wiggly" with the children and supplied them with coloring books and crayons. We rested. We read. And we cooked.

What cooking!

That wood stove!

I loved it—even this temperamental antique! There was a slight disadvantage because the stove was so old that the closing of the oven door brought down a shower of rust on whatever I crowded into it. No matter! We told each other that the slight crunchiness was a pleasant addition and anyway, didn't people need more iron? I must admit that my devotion to wood stoves might have suffered an eclipse if I hadn't had a hungry and patient husband who split wood and dumped ashes.

During the war one of the palatial homes up on the hill became housing for a Coast Guard Beach Patrol Unit. For a while, their war-dogs were tethered in what was once the salon of the hotel—now open to the sky. Aside from the wanton vandalism of the grand piano and the chinaware, the banisters, stairs, birds-eye maple paneling and even parts of the flooring had been chopped for firewood. This desecration was obvious as more and more rooms became exposed to the elements and parts of the once-grand building toppled over the high cliff into the sea below.

Of course our first stay at Bayocean was in desperation for *any place* to rest as earlier recounted, but we became

attached to Bayocean by the reverse of what Mr. Mitchell hoped for. Bayocean was so peaceful. The cottages, sheltered by a wooded rise, separated us from the ocean's frequent blasts of sharp winds even in summer. Sometimes we brought friends with us who also appreciated the solitude and whose children delighted, as did ours, in going "belly-whoppering" down the steep dunes in an old dish pan. We never had to write for reservations.

But Bayocean's best was none too good. When it rained the cabins leaked. To remedy this we were offered apologies and dishpans. A collapsed chair brought an apology along with a replacement from a vacant cottage. When the toilet decided to run day and night and a new manager could only watch it then sadly walk away, my husband drove into Tillamook to a hardware store, bought parts and fixed it.

Through the years the Mitchells watched the deflowering of their dreams. Each winter's storms washed away more of their territory and nobody would help them. Those two old people, stooped with age, indomitably tried to reconstruct the washed out portions of the road with wheelbarrow and shovel. The old gentleman—and gentleman he surely was—was of the stuff with which crusaders and martyrs are made.

The ocean was now undermining most of the great dune which separated Cottage Park from the ocean.

SHIELD - A PAIR OF LEGS, DRAWN AND QUARTERED ON A FIELD OF ROCKS.

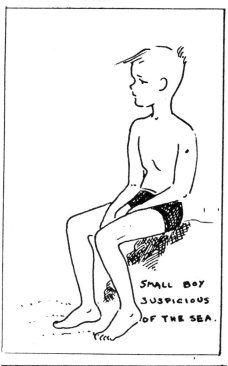

SMALL BOY SUSPICIOUS OF THE SEA.

"TIDE POOLS CAN BE EXCITING—

"THIS IS THE THIRD TIME HE'S LAID HIS HOTDOG DOWN ON THE SAND!"

F. D. Mitchell surveys damage at Jackson Gap, 1948. A resident of Bayocean since 1907, he could often be seen trying to repair the damaged spit with shovel and wheelbarrow.

Although we normally made our annual trips in August, I recall a short trip to Bayocean in October 1952.

When we visited that October, I recall now that the Mitchells had moved into the kitchen of their old Bay Hotel. He was all of eighty—she a year younger. I'll never forget our last chat with them. She, trudging around the room with a thin smile, poured coffee for us. He, with a trace of artificiality in his former verve, had to prod his waning enthusiasm to keep it from melting into the floor. In repose, his face was sad. He looked like a bewildered child who had been punished for some infraction he did not understand. He would gladly sell his holding for a fraction if he could only interest someone with influence. There was this tract of land (he got out an old, soiled and creased map)—let it go for $100 an acre if it would be developed. Or how about this site for $25? Help!...Somebody help!...Anybody?

His fervor was somehow diminished by half a lifetime spent battling both the authorities and the elements. The Mitchells had willed all their property to a church for a

"JUST A FEW THINGS WE'RE TAKING HOME WITH US"

children's camp and pointed with pride to a magnificent refrigerator which their beneficiaries had presented in appreciation. He still had enough spirit to quote a verse of his own composition:

> In nineteen-fifty one
>> We've got them on the run
> In nineteen-fifty two
>> They'll be through
> In nineteen-fifty three
>> We'll be free!

Just how prophetic this doggerel was is tragically evident because by 1953 they were free indeed. After the big break, winter storms continued to pound and the gap widened to nearly one mile with water over the land even at low time. Just before this time a newspaper printed a picture of a fellow standing in front of Mitchell's old store where there was a sign reading, **WATCH BAYOCEAN GROW**.

But in the photograph the man held his hands over the **R** and the **W**, making it read: **WATCH BAYOCEAN G O**.

I guess we were the last persons to inhabit (rent) any of the cabins, for just a few weeks later it was all over. The spit broke under the pounding of an early winter storm and the long narrow neck of Bayocean Spit was broken. The north end of the spit became an island separated from the land to the south by a mile of unrestrained, roaring ocean.

In 1953, Bayocean was inaccessible so we vacationed at Oceanside. Parts of Oceanside were also in satisfactorily dilapidated condition—a little moldy and mildewed and not ordinarily frequented by fashionable people. Once when I asked what happened to the Mitchells, I was told they refused to leave until Mrs. Mitchell had a stroke. It was reported that Mr. Mitchell spent a couple of days trying to signal the mainland for help when finally a Coast Guard boat picked them up.

☆   ☆   ☆

Mrs. Mitchell died in the Tillamook Hospital shortly after she and her husband left Bayocean. Although Mr. Mitchell had taken a room in Tillamook, in reality he could no longer look after himself. He was removed by court order and given a bed in the State Hospital at Salem.

Mitchell had been a man with a dream. A big dream. As a relatively young man when he arrived at Bayocean, he obviously subscribed to the notion that success would come to him if he believed enough in his dream and if he took action to make his dream come true. Although Mitchell faced many challenges, he set out to overcome opposition. He was a living declaration that "Tough Times Never Last, But Tough People Do!" He was a "Possibility Thinker!" He never gave up!

Francis Drake Mitchell died in Salem, Oregon, July 25, 1965. He had lived 95 years, 6 months, and 7 days.

He and his wife are buried in a cemetery at Tillamook, Oregon. □

Francis Drake Mitchell was the first to purchase property at Bayocean and the first to erect a hotel there. This Bayside Hotel was apparently opened in 1908 and brought in instant profits as T. B. Potter's larger hotel, which faced the ocean, took longer to build. In picture, see the dock with its track for Bayocean Railroad, Mitchell's hotel and in back of hotel, across Bay Blvd., is Mitchell's store under construction. Mitchell was a patriot and flew his 45-star American flag daily.

Black line approximates shore line in 1917. Cape Meares Community, lower left. Breakwater, completed in 1956, runs from Pitcher Point, center right, to parking lot approximately one mile from Pitcher Point. Former Bayocean town center is about 850 yards beyond parking lot.

CHAPTER 12

"FIX THE SPIT!"

We recall the role of the U.S. Army Corps of Engineers was specifically *not* in "rebuilding sand dunes, people's front yards, roads of access, or for the benefit of oyster farmers." But now that Bayocean Spit's neck was broken, the movement of sand was clogging the main channel from the ocean into Tillamook Bay. With this menace to navigation well noted, the Army Engineers had a legal reason to finally work on the "Bayocean Problem." The Corps moved in!

A breakwater, if constructed on the basis of the 1950 economy, would cost more than the original proposed priced of a south jetty which the people turned down long ago. The people in The Tillamook-Bay City area were genuinely alarmed and feared the ocean would lap directly onto their low farm lands with risk of inundating theses lands with salt water.

The Beach Erosion Board, along with much public input, announced a plan to build a breakwater. The location would be several hundred yards east of the original neck of the spit and there were sound reasons for this. A major reason was the belief that erosion would continue until a second jetty was constructed. To place the breakwater further east would at least buy time.

After careful consideration, it was decided the break-water would run from Pitcher Point to the "island." This was a straight line as well as slightly shorter than the length of the original neck of the spit.

We remember there was no hard evidence, at this time, that the old north jetty had caused the erosion although this was suspected in some official circles and rumored heavily among the populace. Much talk centered around a suspected need for a south jetty but the Corps was firm that the first

The Bayside (Bay) Hotel, Mitchell Bldg., and other buildings long abandoned and severely vandalized, all in the way of the Corps of Engineers' reclamation project were bulldozed into rubble then burned.

objective was to plug the break by building a breakwater. A south jetty could be considered later.

A breakwater, the Corps of Engineers announced, would cost $1,750,000. The people backed their local governments to subscribe their share for the project and urged the Corps to move ahead quickly.

The work got underway with the Corp awarding a contract. The contractor moved in heavy equipment. The plan called for sluicing in thousands of tons of sand from the bottom of Tillamook Bay and refilling the Main Gap. Many of the old town buildings were pretty ramshackle and were considered to be dangerous. Quite a few were in the way of the proposed landfill so plans were made to wreck them. Bulldozers knocked over the old frame buildings then heaped the debris into huge piles. What a bonfire! (There had been only a handful of people still living there and these were moved off the island.) By now, nearly 98 percent of a once-thriving resort town had been obliterated from the face of the earth. While the breakwater was still under construction with huge trucks moving in heavy rock and gravel, other workers were carefully planting beach grass for a dunes stabilization program which had proven successful elsewhere along the northwest coast. In time, the peninsula was reestablished via the breakwater.

Bonfire (top) quickly consumed debris from old buildings. Mrs. Bennett's daffodils (center, left) bloomed their last in 1972. By the next spring they had fallen into the sea. Remains (right) of Louis Bennett's garage, in spring 1972. By spring 1989, wild strawberry plants were sprawling their way across the spit along with Scotch Broom and tall grass.

Strowger house, which had been on corner of Bay Blvd. and Seal Street, Bayocean, Oregon, slid down the dune then crashed on the then rocky beach when incoming tides undermined its foundation. Wreck was during winter 1953-54 after the grand washout of November 1952.

Louis Bennett visits Bayocean exhibit at Netarts Beachcombers Festival 1973, points toward board salvaged by authors from his garage.

Several homes, which were out of the way of the rebuilding project, but now abandoned, were left to await destruction by forthcoming winter storms. Finally, on February 15, 1960, Burford Wilkerson, a local resident and noted photographer, made a picture as that last house poised on the edge of the dune ready for its plunge to the beach below. But one more building stood—Louis Bennett's garage! Bennett's garage remained the sole building (and used as a checkpoint in our study) for several years, then it too, became undermined and piece-by-piece fell off the cliff. By the spring of 1970 the walls of the small one-car structure had gone. Only the arched roof remained with a corner of this hanging over the edge. When the authors returned in March 1971, about half the roof remained. Our trip there one year later revealed only a few boards left. But there was something else! Years earlier, Mrs. Bennett had planted a row of daffodils by the side of the garage. Now these flowers were on the very edge of the precipice. We

Trail (top) through over-6-foot tall Scotch Broom near parking lot is often shared with horse and mule enthusiasts (center) on weekends. Group (lower) has parked trailers, mounted their animals and are ready for Sunday ride Apr. 30, 1989.

photographed the daffodils then salvaged a board from the garage remains. The board was "Rainbow Girls Blue" as the girls had painted it decades earlier.

At our request, Buck Sherwood visited the area in early 1973 then wrote: "The daffodils are not in evidence." The storms had taken them as well as the last boards from Bennett's garage during the winter.

Today one can drive to Bayocean Park on the new breakwater. The route to Bayocean is west on Tillamook's Third Street (the Netarts-Oceanside Highway). After crossing the Tillamook River, one takes the right fork and drives along the edge of Tillamook Bay—Lockwood's original route—to Pitcher Point. At this point, on the right, is a sign and the start of the two-level driveway out the breakwater to the parking lot near the old town site. (The only "heavy traffic" may be on weekends when local folks haul their horses in trailers to the parking lot, then ride the horses on the peninsula away from the threat of motor vehicles.) The parking lot is on the bay side of the reconstructed spit. The lot is fenced with railroad rails. There is a locked gate on the north side of the lot. The return to the main highway is along the top (west side) of the breakwater about twenty feet above sea level.)

T. B. Potter's "Atlantic City of the West" is hardly visible today. The sluiced-in sand is now mostly covered with beach grass and Scotch Broom.

In 1972 a short length of a "driveway'" (High Street) could be found but in spring 1989 only pieces of its rubble can be found here and there on the beach. Until about 1983, one could find, at low tide, a length of pipe, six inches in diameter protruding from the wet sand. This pipe, with pump attached, once served as a well for the Hicks house. In 1989 no trace of the pipe was found. ☐

Remains of High Street (right) as it appeared in 1972. (Below) Field researcher Dale Webber surveys Bayocean beach during incoming tide. (Right page) Tree with cross-arm for power lines, once served Tent City, was on beach until 1975.

Umpqua River Navigation Company, contractors for construction of South Jetty at Tillamook (Bayocean) Spit, used giant-sized trucks to haul enormous "Class A" rocks to be fit closely into new jetty like pieces in a jig-saw puzzle.

CHAPTER 13

TILLAMOOK SPIT GETS ITS SOUTH JETTY

The long-awaited south jetty was approved under the River and Harbors Act of 1965. Umpqua River Navigation Company received the bid. The new jetty would extend from Kincheloe Point over one mile into the ocean. While older jetties had been constructed by running a light railroad over the tops of the rocks as the rocks were dumped, the modern era dictated this be a motor truck and crane job. Along with heavy equipment, the contractor installed shack offices on the lee side of the Point. Pacific Northwest Bell Telephone Company dug a trench and buried subterranean cable on the spit for the benefit of the Corp of Engineers and the contractor.

(This telephone line is a single "E" wire which runs from a terminal near the intersection of the highway from Tillamook and the breakwater road [sometimes called Bayocean Road], out the breakwater to the end of the spit. The circuit was intended as temporary for use during the building of the South Jetty. Now that the jetty is completed, the line is idle.)

(Based on distance from the telephone office, a single "E" wire is capable of carrying up to four different numbers operating as a "party line," but could carry nearly 100 numbers if special adapters were added. This telephone line is the only "utility" presently installed on Bayocean Spit.)

Will a second jetty at the Tillamook entrance stop erosion of the spit? Aerial photos made during jetty construction show sand building up (accretion) along the northwest corner of Kincheloe Point between the jetty and the point—solid beach rebuilding. But to the south, west of the breakwater, erosion has continued, but not a great annual rate, to the present time.

It took about three decades of erosion to break the spit. How long will it take to rebuild Bayocean's frontage—the beautiful long and wide beach? Scientists have not tried to guess but the fact is very clear, the beach is rebuilding.

When we searched records to see if anyone still owned property at Bayocean in 1973, we were amazed to learn many did. With the assistance of the Tillamook County Assessor, we located over fifty properties then on tax rolls. Some were under water and people wouldn't believe it! In 1982 when the authors again asked officials about the status of property on the spit, we learned people still had lots there —48 properties. The owners were near and far—local Tillamook to Virginia. But none were found in Kansas City, Potter's original mid-west promotion ground.

Why do people keep lots in a place like Bayocean? Some say their lot was willed to them "and it wouldn't be right to part with it." Others hold property in perpetual trust. Some law firms hold property as parts of unsettled estates. One woman said, "It belonged to my parents and as a child I grew up there. Our land was not totally taken by the ocean and someday I believe it will all come back. The taxes are minimal and I just want to keep it."

Some lots are west of a zone line and do not pay any taxes or carry any value, according to the Tillamook County Assessor. Others have only a small value due to limitations.

What about building a summer cabin on your lot at Bayocean Spit? County officials were quick to point out that all construction requires permits. The Assessor's office wrote, "No developing or construction is allowed in the area by the Zoning, Planning or Sanitation Departments [but the telephone line is in]." It's these limitations which hold taxes down.

Is there a master plan for developing the spit again? Apparently not, due to the moratorium on permits. Can anyone who owns property there spend a weekend in a tent or camper? Camping permits are not issued because of no sanitation facilities. Even if this challenge could be met, it would be a long walk with a heavy load from the parking lot to one's site—if one could find his site as there are no easy-to-identify markers on the land. As to recreational vehicles, even the self-contained models, the county says no. (The breakwater road and the lot are patrolled by the Sheriff. Those with campers who want to research the spit will find hookups at Barview County Park or at Cape Lookout State Park but only if this park, now suffering severe ocean erosion, does not, itself, succumb.) ☐

Margie Webber with object found in tall beach grass.

121

Sally (above left) and Dale Webber (right), "beachcombing" for artifacts from town of Bayocean in 1982. (Below) Sally, on unimproved trail through beach grass between parking lot and beach.

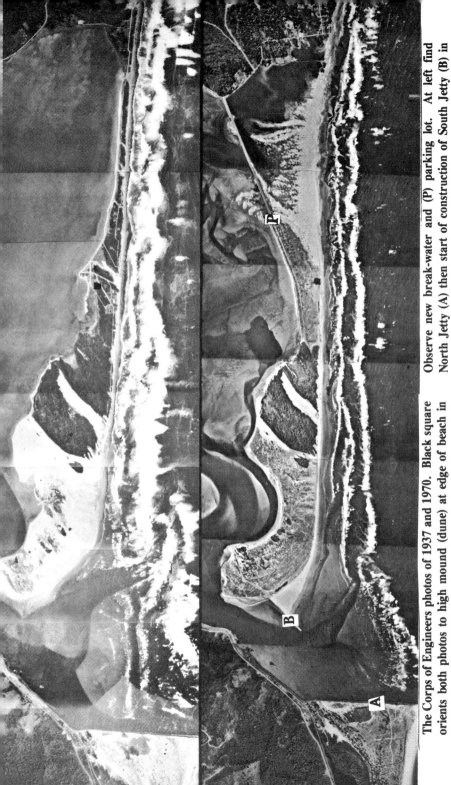

The Corps of Engineers photos of 1937 and 1970. Black square orients both photos to high mound (dune) at edge of beach in 1983. Remains of High Street near here. In top picture at right note road from Tillamook to Cape Meares Community.

Observe new break-water and (P) parking lot. At left find North Jetty (A) then start of construction of South Jetty (B) in lower photo. South Jetty is now finished.

BAYOCEAN IS A FUN PLACE. Experienced hikers at Bayocean recommend visitors carry water, snack and always a jacket. Be careful, remembering there are no telephones and no help for many miles.

CHAPTER 14

BAYOCEAN TODAY

Camera faces south with Tillamook Bay on left, Pacific Ocean, right. Acres of beach grass and Scotch broom hold sand in place. Few artifacts of the once-grand resort can be found here as area shown is largely "fill" sluiced in from bottom of Tillamook Bay. Unimproved road, closed to public, was access to South Jetty construction area. Although some people still own property here, no building or camping is permitted primarily because of lack of sanitation. There is no power or water but "Ma Bell" has installed a subterranean telephone cable. Cape Meares in distance. Beach grass (right) in 1989, has thrived to a point where officials are transplanting to some other areas along the Oregon coast. Camera faces northwest from parking lot. Kincheloe Point in distance. □

125

BAYOCEAN PENINSULA
USGS Chart No. 6112

Official charts cover 81-year period showing the narrowing then broken spit followed by peninsula reestablishment by Corps of Engineers breakwater project. Bayocean Park resort community once called the "million dollar playground of the west," now gone except for a few pieces of cobble-driveways one might beachcomb at low tide. Drawings based on U.S. Geodetic Survey Chart No. 6112, not to scale.

Tillamook Bay entrance May 31, 1989. Camera faces northwest. (Top) (A) North Jetty, 1917, rebuilt 1933. (B) South Jetty, 1983. (C) Sand deposit robbed from eroding Tillamook Spit starting about 1917. (D) Sand buildup against new South Jetty. (E) Kincheloe Point. (F) Jetty access road closed to public. (G) (Lower) Public parking lot. (H) Public access driveways to parking lot.

House Falls Off
Salishan Spit

By United Press International

A house fell into the ocean off Salishan Spit Thursday as winds, heavy rains and high tides hit the coast.

The house under construction dropped into the water after the sea eroded the bank on which it was being built, residents of the area said. [For location, see mape page 143]

CHAPTER 15

SALISHAN

There are several potential washout areas along the Northwest Coast, particularly in Oregon. The Oregon coast contains no less than fifteen estuaries, many with a spit of sand which guards the bay. When certain conditions prevail long enough, any of these spits may be subject to partition.

Potter promoted the building of an entire town along with palatial homes on Tillamook (Bayocean) Spit. In recent years a troupe of promoters have planted buildings, mostly homes, on the sands of other spits. By 1970, there were dozens of expensive homes and several condominiums on Siletz Spit—popularly called Salishan Spit.

The spit protects Siletz Bay, a waterway used by pleasure boats, but at this time without commercial significance, at the south edge of Lincoln City. The entrance channel is narrow and frequently changes, limiting the depth at high tide some years to only about three feet at the bar. There are no jetties at the entrance of this bay. Nevertheless, during the Christmas season 1972, rip currents, along with high tides driven by brute-force winds, eroded the fore dune and threatened some homes. People spent a lot of time and money hauling rock which was dumped between their homes and the ocean. Some occupants along the spit were steadfast in their statements: "We believe our homes to be very safe," but some moved anyway.

Salishan's first "victim" was a $60,000 house under construction on lot No. 226. Pounding breakers ate the sand dune, undermined house thus building tumbled. Geoffrey Madden, in 1973 editor of *Lincoln City News-Guard*, visited spit January 18, 1973 to photograph this house then perched at edge of bluff. Of a number of pictures he made, view shown was taken while the house slid over the edge to the beach below. Within one week all the frame work was gone leaving only the concrete foundation, that had been poured on sand, on the beach. In another year even the foundation had vanished.

129

Bayocean

The authors started a study of Salishan Spit in mid-1972. (The popular Salishan Lodge is nearby, but not on the spit.) Access to the spit by car is strictly monitored, as the land above the state-owned beach is all private property. One can walk along the spit, avoiding the private entrance, by entering through Gleneden Beach State Park about one mile to the south. Early into our research we made contact with the Oregon Department of Geology and Mineral Industries as personnel from that agency had recently made official observations on the spit. To our inquiry came the reply, "With regard to the Salishan matter, I can state on the basis of my reconnaissance investigations of the spit, that at first glance it does not appear to be one of the more stable areas along the coast. Equating it with Bayocean is most perceptive of you." Later, a newspaper quoted the geologist who declared: "I would not build a house there."

Just a few days later, Christmas holiday residents and visitors along the spit were forced into a royal battle against the sea. A winter storm challenged the palatial homes, many valued at more than half-a-million dollars. On Christmas Eve 1972, the battering was in earnest.

A house under construction (lot No. 226) near the edge of the dune toppled over the fifteen-foot cliff and onto the beach below. Within a week there were no signs of the building other than a few pieces of scrap concrete, which had been the foundation, littering the beach.

The front page of the *Oregon Journal* (Portland) for December 28, 1972, gave this account:

Monster waves fanned by heavy Southwest winds and high tides are threatening homes on Salishan Spit, the 2½-mile strip of sand dunes and driftwood separating the Pacific from Siletz Bay.

An around-the-clock battle against erosion is under way and at least three expensive homes and thousands of dollars in beach property are threatened. Salishan Properties spokesmen point out.

Christmas Eve three homes were set to topple onto the beach when the tide knifed away more than 20 feet of gently sloping property, leaving the houses, owned by Portlanders, perched on the edge of crumbling sand and logs.

The damaged homes are owned by Millard Cohn, Gordon Paulson and Leon Savaria.

Despite holiday difficulties, Bob Houston, Jr., Houston Construction Co., Seal Rock, recruited men, equipment and rock, most of which came from Yaquina head.

Work started around 10 a.m. Christmas Eve and is still under way, dumping rock over the steep bank with other equipment pushing the boulders into place at low tide.

In the meantime the property owners north and south of the three homes are threatened.

Other homes have been protected from similar erosion, a winter hazard. It is estimated that several hundred thousand dollars has been spent in the last three years.

Alex Murphy, Salishan Lodge Manager, who lives nearby, points out that the problem exists anywhere homes are built on an exposed beach.

"It is something all such property owners realize exists. If anything, we have wider, clearer beaches and additional tons of driftwood!

Newspapers were full of stories and feature articles. People demanded that the Corps of Engineers "fix the spit." The State was blamed. The Governor went on record saying no state funds would be used to prop up sagging front yards built of sand.

Eric W. Allen, Jr., editor of the *Medford Mail Tribune* editorialized in 1972:

GLENEDEN BEACH, Ore. It has become overwhelmingly obvious in recent years that industrialized man is capable of changing the environment in ways he did not intend to do simply because he didn't know any better.

One example among many is man's work on spits, estuaries and beaches. It still is not thoroughly understood, although more is being learned.

For instance, the construction of a jetty into the ocean, built to protect the inlet and provide access to it by ships and boats, can change the character of a whole section of coastline, simply by changing ocean currents along the shore and thus the pattern in which sand is deposited on the beaches.

Construction of upriver dams on major waterways can, by blocking the flow of natural sediments (principally sand) change the character of beaches.

Particularly vulnerable to such changes are spits, which are nothing more than sand dunes that have been built across the mouths of rivers, forming a beach on the outer side and a bay on the inner side. Such spits are fragile things, and change in shape, contour, and length with the whim of tide and storm and flood— and also because of changes wrought by man.

This lesson should have been learned by the fate of a promotional-development town known as Bayocean, which was built on the spit that separated Tillamook Bay from the ocean, and which simply washed away [after a series of breaks, the worst being in 1952].

But the lesson was not learned. The spit which creates Siletz Bay here is the site of a large number of expensive homes, part of the beautiful Salishan development. Now that they have been built, some of their occupants are beginning to worry about the constantly shifting sands, particularly since a storm some months ago changed the entire configuration of the seaward beach.

Other man-made changes in the estuary itself, including fills and berms and dikes, have also caused changes in currents in the bay, which is resulting in erosion on the inner side of the spit.

(This page) Home of Millard Cohn once was about 30 feet from bluff, had front yard of attractive beach grass but was suddenly threatened by the sea. Mrs. Cohn assured authors she felt her home was secure. See location (F) at right. (Right page) Corps of Engineers photo of Siletz (Salishan) Spit Feburary 8, 1973 looking north: (A) Ocean; (B) Siletz Bay; (C) Salishan Drive from Highway 101; (D) Lagoon connecting Siletz Bay; (E) Embayment caused by rip tides; (F) Rip rap (rocks, etc.) dumped in front of selected properties in attempt to stop erosion; (G) Driftwood deposited by one tide may be totally washed away on next tide; (H) Salishan Condos.

Bayocean

> Residents are, understandably, concerned. And, with an investment well in excess of one million dollars on the spit alone, they are determined that the Bayocean story will not be repeated. We hope they are right, and that the lesson—that the effects of man's works are often unpredictable—sinks in. E.A.

Within a few days the authors responded to Editor Allen's editorial with these remarks after recapping the Bayocean history:

> Any determination the residents of Siletz (Salishan) Spit have today about keeping the ocean away seems a little late. The literature shows that the Corps of Engineers did not, in the past, cotton to the idea of shoring up residential beaches against erosion. It would appear real estate developers will sell anything and develop anything that people will buy and apparently neither the public nor the realtors do much homework [when it's beach property with concern for potential erosion by the sea].
>
> Recently the entire Planning Commission of Tillamook County was asked to resign over sand area development ideas promoted by realtors.
>
> As a conclusion based on research, we feel the people of Salishan have a very real problem. We feel for them indeed, but with a very long stick and with us perched upon much firmer ground.

At Salishan, all the home owners did not subscribe to the plan for fronting their property with "riprap" as they called it—dump truck loads of large rocks, gravel and *sand!* While the rock piles thwarted the sea from frontal attacks for a short while, the ocean boiled in and around the ends of the "riprap" then churned further inland.

Contractors hauled more filler to be dumped in front of homes all the next season. The people who lived on the spit had to pay for it.

Within a week of the loss of the house, an unrelated incident occurred which soon made headlines and forced additional attention to Salishan's beaches.

The new ferro-concrete schooner *Marjean* was launched and was on her maiden trip having cast off from the little dock at Taft, just inside the entrance of Siletz Bay.

The skipper-owner set his course for the ocean and entered the channel *on an incoming tide.* Just over the bar his small engine quit. Heavy seas forced the now helpless 48-foot long yacht onto the beach where the occupants jumped off the ship onto the beach, then walked to the nearest house for help.

The incoming high tide hurled telephone pole-size logs that cracked the hull. In addition, the sand around the heavy ship was rapidly washing away from the hull with each receding wave. Authorities feared this erosion would work its way along the beach, so ordered the owner to remove the schooner by whatever means—quickly. Apparently the only means available was a bulldozer. The 'dozer scraped out a pit in the beach, smashed the hull, then pushed the rubble into the hole and covered it with sand. A Marine Inspector reported the loss at $100,000. The owners, who had envisioned a round-the-world cruise on *Marjean,* stayed home.

The hull of the schooner, having been on the beach for just a few days, created a small embayment which was visible for nearly one year. Sometimes, if one walks to a certain spot toward the end of the spit a little northwest of the last house, one might find reinforcing wire from the *Marjean* protruding from the sand.

☆   ☆   ☆

Dumping "riprap" on Siletz Spit, January 1973.

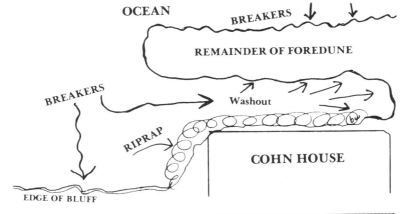

OCEAN

BREAKERS

REMAINDER OF FOREDUNE

BREAKERS

Washout

RIPRAP

COHN HOUSE

EDGE OF BLUFF

(Opposite, top) Riprap (rocks) dumped in front of house between tides, then next high tide undermined porch causing it to collapse. In frenzy, contractor dismantled porch, dumping more rock. Several tides later, 20-foot high foredune had disappeared. (Opposite, lower) January 23, 1973, Margie views high tide from porch—now with guardrail. (This page, top to bottom) By May 1973 ocean had redeposited sand, covered rocks. House has rebuilt porch then later appears vacant. Margie observes beach grass stabilized dune on April 30, 1989. Will ocean chew up this site again?

"The best way to ruin a perfectly good day is to wreck your ship." *Marjean*, 48-foot ferro-cement schooner hard aground on Siletz Spit, became total loss. The ship was on its maiden voyage.

By February 1973, when the authors measured one of their check-points on Siletz Spit, there was about 100 feet remaining between the high tide line and a lagoon which branches from Siletz Bay near "lot 226." Would the last of the high tides of the winter breach the spit here? If not, how about the storms in following winters? In the meantime, farther out on the spit, a contractor was pouring mortar on the sand for another house!

Studies have determined that winter erosion usually occurs as a result of a series of rough storms rather than from a single storm. Rip currents, and a series of high tides, driven by sharp winds, eat away at the beach and carry sand out to sea. When the beach is gone, the next storms pound directly on the dune line, chewing up the dune. As the dune disintegrates, if there is a building on it, the foundation of the building is undermined and the building tumbles to the beach below. (On the northwest coast it would be a rare occurrence for a breaker to actually hit a building and knock it down.)

The possibility for erosion occurs if a rip current remains in one place along the beach pulling sand from the beach with each receding wave. When a rip stays in one place, a beach can be eroded to where the area resembles a small bay (embayment). If the condition continues, this embayment may reach the foredunes.

Driftwood along the Northwest Coast contributes to dune stability as well as to dune destruction. Consider large logs tossed high onto the beach during a severe storm. When the logs stay put—do not roll back on the receding wave— they may be covered with wind-driven sand during non-storm periods during summers. These logs tend to stabilize and reinforce the dune. But logs, especially during wild winter storms, also act as battering rams, as in the case of the destruction of the *Marjean*.

Home and motel owners who have buildings on the

Margie Webber starts hike along Salishan Spit during field trip concerned with coastal erosion and beachcombing. Pack sack contains food bars, extra pants, socks, shoes. Interesting driftwood plus any stray Japanese glass fishing floats will be brought back.

Even while the arguments were going on about liability for erosion, a contractor was preparing foundation for another house (top, left). A year later, the house (top, right) was completed. With camera on beach facing house (center), observe driftwood that had been hurled from the sea. Do catapulting logs pose threat to sleepers in such houses on wild, stormy nights? Construction has continued along Siletz Spit on a regular basis. New start (lower) photographed April 30, 1989.

140

dunes or on the beach have had to learn the hard way about driftwood and winter storms. Not infrequently do huge logs crash through ocean frontage windows with the potential of becoming an uninvited bed partner for one who might have designed his bedroom facing the "beautiful" ocean! Some motels along the central Oregon coast do not rent their first floor, ocean-facing rooms during winter storms due to this threat. Logs may be heaved high on the beach during one high tide and storm combination, then picked up and taken back to sea on the next.

A storm system developed during February 1976 and the ocean again chose Salishan. Off-shore rips had caused embayments along the spit in two places. One was near the center of the spit and the other was farther out adjacent to the most northerly building. These embayments set the stage for a wild storm which would overwash Salishan Spit on February 18th. As the breakers approached the spit there was no longer a beach upon which they could dissipate so the water rushed on without breaking or losing energy until near the shoreline. When the breakers hit the dunes near the end of the spit, logs which had been deposited earlier were shoved ahead of the water to a point where huge piles of other logs and stumps had been deposited in 1960. But this

Huge stump tossed by an angry ocean was left on the bay-side of the spit during 1976 washover.

time waves continued across this "1960 line" leaving logs in a so-called wash-over pond near Salishan Drive. The water continued over the road and crashed into Siletz Bay. But even with this washover, the spit held.

During the decade of 1972-82, the beach and fore dune in mid-spit underwent significant changes. As earlier mentioned, when the house under construction toppled near here in 1972, the cliff from which it fell was about fifteen feet high. Contractors poured tons of riprap along the area but much of this became eroded during the next few winters. The riprap largely disappeared.

We might take a minute to discuss riprap. Some define this as loosely applied rocks to form a foundation. Others place the rock in a close-fitting scheme as in a jig-saw puzzle to make a foundation very firm. Still others use a "tetrapod" concrete structure, each tetrapod slightly resembling a gigantic "jack" as in "Jacks, a children's game played with a bouncing ball." Tetrapods placed together to form a foundation may appear to move slightly under pressure so as to force them together when struck by a wave. (To the authors' knowledge, the only tetrapod installation along the northwest coast is at Crescent City, California.)

Riprap applied at Salishan consisted, as witnessed and photographed by the authors, of dump truck loads of large rocks, gravel and sand which seemed to be unceremoniously dumped along a predetermined line. Then a crane moved some of the larger rocks. As reported in a publication of Oregon State University Extension Marine Advisory Program (SG 35):

> Some riprap in front of Siletz [Salishan] homes...has... fallen away because of powerful wave action, faulty riprap construction, and the use of rocks too small to be effective.

The authors "watch" certain areas on the spit each spring and make photos of beach changes. We have been doing this for nearly two decades. During the on-site observations, we have seen a firming of the foredune in one

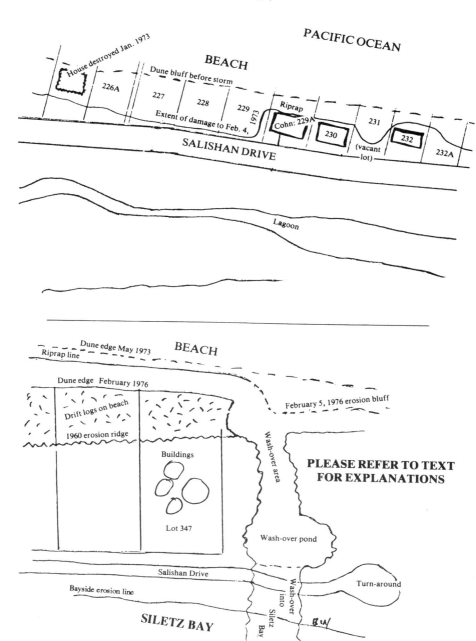

Drift logs weighing hundreds of pounds are hurled upon beaches during high tides in winter storm period. Very unstable, these logs are dangerous for beachcombers to jump on, often roll under pressure—may be carried back to sea on next tide.

area following the winter 1972 devastation when wave action appears to have pushed the riprap closer together. Then followed a period of destruction. The 1976 storm which did wash over the spit near the outer end, beveled the foredune in mid-spit. When we photographed the area in 1982, the riprap and the dune was gone and a tapered sand beach extended from the high tide line to Salishan Drive—the spit's only access road.

One of our points of reference is a certain house owned in 1972 by Millard Cohn. (This house has been mentioned earlier. See photos and map.) We also look for a specific fire hydrant along the side of the road. At one time the dune was as much as four feet higher than the fire plug. Then a storm leveled the dune to where the hydrant was again on the skyline. Did high winter tides during 1981-82 sweep over

Beautiful Siletz (Salishan) Spit viewed from hill in Taft area of Lincoln City. Entrance to Siletz Bay in foreground during ebb tide.

the road and into the lagoon? The distance is only a few feet, and all "down grade" from the road into the lagoon. Scientists the authors talked with do not agree a washover occurred near the Cohn house (lot No. 229-A) at this time. But when the authors were on site in 1982, Salishan Drive, in this area, was covered with about half-an-inch of sand. Beach grass, planted in an attempt the stabilize the dunes was "bent" and leaned toward the lagoon.

The authors suggest that a high tide during the winter 1981-82 roared up the slanted beach, bent the grass, covered the road with sand, then flowed into the lagoon! A washover!

The authors have observed that most of those living on

the spit are generally quiet about happenings there.

Questions come to mind: When can high waves be expected? How high must a storm wave be to cause damage?

Along the Northwest Coast, high tides and severe winds occur primarily between November and March. During those months, breakers average between nine and twelve feet in contrast to summer conditions when breaker heights average three to six feet high. In December of 1972, when the Christmas Eve parties were interrupted along Salishan Spit, the sea was throwing breakers about *21 feet high* against the dunes. Komer and McKinney reported in 1976 these were the highest wave conditions observed between November 1971 and 1976, since the microseismometer system was installed at the Marine Science Center at Newport, Oregon, in November 1971.

What was the cause of the erosion at Salishan?

Rip current embayments cut into foredunes when high tides and severe storms smashed the dunes, then the sand was carried out to sea. A sand mining operation just south of the spit may have deprived the spit of a source of sand normally brought to the beach by northbound, alongshore (Davidson) current.

Do people fear the sea? This Salishan Spit house on "stilts" is just a few feet from where a house fell over the bluff onto the beach in 1973. When the house was finished, builder closed in the pilings. Front of house, facing ocean, shown.

Historically, Siletz Spit has been subject to varying cycles of erosion and accretion. During the 1972-73 winter, several homeowners privately feared a breach in the spit would occur. As we have seen, one house under construction was lost and riprap was placed in front of others. Continuing storms cut around the ends of riprap which had been placed in front of some properties, requiring more rock be dumped on each side of some houses. In the case of the Cohn house, one could originally stand on the front deck and view the ocean beyond a front yard of beach grass-topped dune over fifty feet wide. By the end of that wild winter, one standing on a now rebuilt deck—part of it collapsed when undermined—looked nearly straight down at crashing breakers pounding at the hastily dumped rock. What to do but pile more and larger rocks in front of a house and along the sides in the hope that the ocean will not undermine it?

Do people fear the sea? Some obviously don't. □

Margie Webber near edge of bluff just south of Nestucca Bay entrance May 1981. Haystack Rock (elev. 327 ft.) on horizon. Dotted line indicated end of spit lost probably during storms of January 26-27, 1983.

CHAPTER 16

NESTUCCA:
A "NATURAL" BREACHING

The February 8-9, 1978, storm, combined with a high tide roared through an embayment caused by riptides and breached Nestucca Spit. One of the breaking waves was measured at slightly over *23 feet high!* Although spit-breaching storms seem to be common along the east and Gulf Coasts, the Nestucca Spit breaching is the first known natural breaching of a spit on the west coast of the United States, according to Paul D. Komar of the School of Oceanography, Oregon State University.

Komar reported on the Nestucca break in a paper prepared under a grant through the Sea Grant College Program at the University.

The winter 1977-78 storms caused trouble all along the beaches of the Pacific Northwest. At Salishan, where the frontage had been fairly well protected by this time by riprapping, there was some property loss but no dwellings

Nestucca: A Natural Breaching

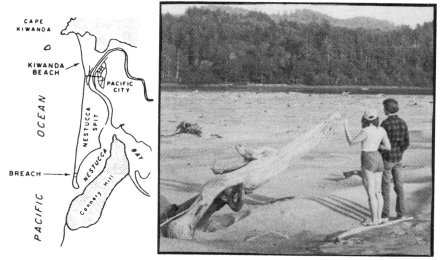

Visitors can reach end of spit by 5-mile round-trip hike, or with 4-wheel drive vehicle on beach—with some risk of being stuck in sand.

fell as a result of the storms. The storms did threaten a number of houses at Pacific City, which is near the base of Nestucca Spit, particularly adjacent to Cape Kiwanda. Reaction to the damage in front of the houses was swift as in earlier years at Salishan. Property owners hired truckers to haul rock to be dumped in their front yards.

Erosion along Nestucca Spit reached from the base all the way to the tip. Some areas were endangered more than others. Rip currents hollowed out the beach, allowing breakers to crash against the dunes. It is difficult to compare Nestucca and Salishan as the sand on Nestucca Spit is considerably finer grained than that found at Salishan. The fine grains lead to wider embayments. At Salishan, the bays were relatively narrower because of the coarser sand.

There is evidence at Nestucca, as found at Salishan, that severe winter storms many years ago washed over the spit, for buried under the dune line are old logs. Natural processes and quiet winters left the logs on the beach—some thrown quite high onto the dunes. These were later covered by wind-driven sand.

Picturesque Nestucca Spit, bay, and Bob Straub State Park, formerly identified as Nestucca Spit State Park, photographed in May 1972. Note several embayments along the spit, the largest in center of picture causing narrowing of the beach. This broke in a storm the night of February 18-19, 1978. Nestucca Spit is the only "natural" breaching anywhere on

the west coast of the United States to the present time. Now, turn the book upside down to view this March 1978 aerial photograph from the pilot's point of view. Beyond entrance to bay is site, on cliff, from which picture on page 148 was made.

In the area of the break at Nestucca, these old logs, now exposed, were inspected and found to be thoroughly rotten.

While there are houses on the spit immediately south of Cape Kiwanda and extending slightly south of Pacific City, there is no development in the area of the break, which is near the tip.

Bob Straub State park comprises all of the spit south of the platted town of Pacific City and west of the Nestucca River and north of the outlet of Nestucca Bay. This is a very large area and occupies most of the spit. Except for a public parking area just south of the limits of Pacific City, a boat launching ramp and public rest rooms, the park is void of buildings.

That the breaching of the spit was not big headlines is understandable considering there were no buildings at risk and no one lived there. The break occurred at one of the two narrower parts of the spit. The slenderest is just south of the county bridge which crosses the river west of Pacific City's town center. The other narrows which breached, is near the tip of the spit (see drawing).

Was there damage to Nestucca Bay from the sudden influx of sand, as happened at Tillamook Bay when the 1952 break there ruined thousands of acres of oyster beds?

Nestucca Bay is largely undeveloped. As mentioned earlier, there is a small boat launching ramp near the center of the spit on the bay side. The bay and the Nestucca River are reported to be good for salmon fishing. As to mollusks, there are no commercial beds here and the softshell clam inhabits an area near the outlet of the Little Nestucca River on a protected arm of the bay well away from the damaged part of the spit.

The sand that entered the bay through the breach spread out over the shallow, muddy bottom in a fan-like manner. As the main channel of the bay is more to the east, the beach sand will probably remain in the relatively still waters of this part of the bay for some time.

Approximately seven weeks after the break, Paul Komar was on the spit to observe water levels which covered the spit at high tide. He reported:

> Under the [approximate 8-foot] high tide of 26 March the breach was intermittently awash. When a series of high waves reached the coast, the breach would become flooded in its central portions to depths of about 110 cm [that is, waist deep, my unfortunate means of measurement]!
>
> There was evidence that the previous night's [approximate 12-foot] high tide, produced considerably more flooding of the breach.

On a subsequent trip in late April, Komar observed the dunes near the high tide line at the north end of the break were being rapidly eroded but those to the south much less. He wrote, "It was this erosion of the ocean-side of the dunes by wave action that mainly accounted for the growing width of the breach..." He pointed out that the sand being washed from the dunes was being carried into the breach—not washed out to sea on receding waves. Thus, as the dunes continued to break down, the beach in front of the broken spit was slowly rebuilding. Komar wrote:

> The development of this breach is very unusual for the coast of Oregon and to the west coast of the United States. The only other reported spit breaching known to have occurred within historic times was at Bayocean...[that] breaching was caused by the construction of a jetty at the entrance of Tillamook Bay and was therefore not entirely natural. The breaching of Nestucca Spit is the only *natural occurrence* [italics added] of sand spit breaching on the west coast of the United States.

There are numerous examples of "washovers" (as Siletz Spit in 1976), particularly on the east and Gulf coasts. Komar contends the lack of spit breachings in the west is because "the west is tectonically rising, in the case of Oregon rising nearly as fast as the present rise in sea level due to glacial melting."

The process of erosion on Nestucca Spit and on Siletz (Salishan) Spit are much the same, where rip current embayments played like roles. Was this the first time Nestucca Spit was breached? Probably not, as the presence of old logs uncovered by the breaching attest.

Nestucca Spit May 31, 1989, 2 p.m.

When the authors visited the breached area in spring of 1981, we found the beach was gradually rebuilding. As we walked over the area, we observed remains of rotten driftwood from an earlier breaching which Komar noted. Probably the most significant evidence that the area was rebuilding, was the sight of many young plants sprouting through the sand. In January 1983 the spit breached again and over 100 yards at the end is gone. Only time will tell if it will rebuild. □

"The Capes" at Oceanside, Oregon

In winter 1998, a locked-gate exclusive community "The Capes," between Netarts and Oceanside, on a high dune overlooking the ocean, was threatened by coastal erosion so severely that many of the houses along the edge of the cliff were ordered vacated by Tillamook County. The restriction was later lifted on some homes, but those most close to the edge of the 100-foot high dune are still threatened. Seasoned observers of sea-caused erosion on the Oregon coast remarked that The Capes, as well as Salishan (Siletz) Spit, was "another Bayocean that could happen any time."

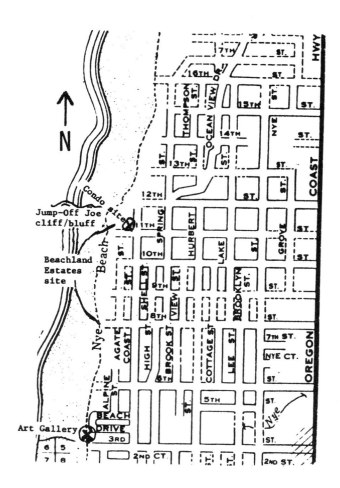

CHAPTER 17

NEWPORT AND JUMP-OFF JOE

Newport, on Oregon's north coast, seems to have been a fishing village—apparently mostly deep-sea fishing—for decades. Today's city continues the tradition with added attractions, including beachside homes and retirement living. But while life goes on, the sea continues an age-old attack on the city's front yard. Although the town got its start along Yaquina Bay, an expanded business section soon perched itself atop a ridge separating the bay and the ocean. The major residential section now occupies the west side of the ridge sloping toward the sea.

Newspaper accounts of "sinking" conditions appeared in 1914. It would seem that the earth suddenly dropped and if there was a building on top of it, the building went into the hole. This was on the western slope near the ocean.

In February 1914, sodden earth wettened by heavy rains, caused a 400-foot long landslide that shoved a seawall into the bay. Then high tides roared into the bay, swept over the sunken wall and eroded away the unprotected roadway. At the same time, on the ocean frontage, a popular area called "Jump-Off Joe" continued to erode at a regular rate as had been observed for years. But most of the homes, as well as a 5-story frame hotel, were either far enough back, or sat high on firm ground—although close to the cliff—so escaped damage.

Between December 1942 and March 1943, Portland newspapers were headlining, "Earth Wiggles Beach Houses; Newport Residents Forced to Move," (*Oregonian*), "House Tumbles Into Widening Gap at Newport; Others Totter," and, "School Teacher's House is Moved" (*Oregon Journal*).

Part of these troubles was the old story of sinking earth that carried buildings with it. One house fell into a crevasse 50 feet wide. Other buildings were reported to be on the edge of a "mysterious hole nearly two blocks long and 20 feet deep" in the Jump-Off Joe area. This condition was along Coast Street where underground activity also undermined a hillside of trees that extended to the bluffs next to the ocean. But between the 100-foot high bluff and the ocean, several houses became marooned by a drop-off to the ocean on one side and the perplexing cavity on the other.

At the same time, along the beach which historically had been narrow, rock formations at the base of the cliff were crumbling under constant pounding by heavy tides. The Army Corps of Engineers advanced a theory that the bluff was being undermined by the sea thereby permitting

House tumbles into widening gap near Jump-Off Joe.

tides to flush out sand under a heavier soil that constituted the bluff. The Corps said this erosion was apparently causing subterranean caverns into which the earth above it, and the buildings thereon, sank. The area concerned was as much as 350 feet from the ocean. Some validation to the army report came from residents who said they observed sand bubbling up in the ocean close inshore during heavy storms.

Erosion-prone areas along a sea-front sometimes have islands of stability. In Newport, the original 1914 building which housed the city recreation room had been built right on the beach. Its foundation and beach-front location closely resemble the old hotel that faces the sea at Cannon Beach (which see). This old Newport building had withstood winter batterings of high tides all these years, the only damage reported being a few broken windows. In 1989 this building is owned by the Yaquina Art Association and serves as a gallery and museum. Louise Lindsay, who has lived just a few blocks from the building for 62 years, and Jeanne Cloe, who also lives close by (46 years) attest to the destructive forces of the winter storm tides along what is called the Nye Beach area. They recall the hassles and dozens of letters to the editor in the Newport *News-Times* when an out-of-town developer decided to perch a 40-unit subdivision on cliffs surrounding Jump-Off Joe bluff.

The developer proclaimed a seawall would hold the land-mass together and keep out the winter high tides. After several months of arguments, Fr. Neil J. Moore, of Newport's Sacred Heart Church wrote:

> Where children used to run and play there is now a giant quagmire. All the trees have been leveled. Not even Attila the ·Hun in all his glory could surpass the pillaging being done there.

The Rev. Moore was shocked at "the pillaging being done at Jump-Off Joe and prayed for mercy for those who are 'crazed by greed'."

Another writer related how:

> A "man"iacal machine is tearing a ravaging swath from the bluff through gentle wooded areas where birds, rabbits, even deer once dwelt by our ocean. Sorry, the roar of the bulldozer spoils the sounds of nature.

Articles appeared in a great crying out against "this ruthless example of 'free enterprise' destruction that should have been zoned for preservation, not for speculative 'development'—to use a most inappropriate designation." Writer Wilmer Froistad, Newport, continued:

> There is something seriously wrong with the planning procedures...that authorizes any kind of conditional approval that has permitted the destruction of another of this community's greatest assets—its attractiveness...

History shows that erosion in the Jump-Off Joe area

Nye Beach frontage walkway and new recreation building (top) in 1914. Heavy breaker (center) blasts building, onlookers in late 1920s. Soon after, the city took out windows and built sturdy wall. The building (lower) still stands solid in spring 1989.

had been going on for decades. Froistad declared:

> The high banks below Coast Street road are continuing to slough-off and the road to the low bench below Jump-Off Joe is the same sort of sandy-clay material.
> Any uninformed buyer who buys [a] building in this area is going to lose his investment, but the developers will have made their profit and moved on.

The developer, on the other hand, announced in a public meeting that it was necessary to clear the land so drains to carry off surface water could be installed. The drains combined with other measures will "theoretically" stop erosion, he said.

Ernie Smith, formerly a civil engineer with the U.S. Army Corps of Engineers, a local resident, wrote:

> The project is doomed to failure due to faulty engineering design. The two dozen more or less engineering experts in the [developers'] group are ridiculing the professional engineers whom they consider mentally retarded. The group is apparently sure they can convince the city officials by reason of their own mental superiority and if not, then will wear them out.

From Oregon State University, Paul Komar of the oceanographic staff, who has made extensive and continuing studies of the coast, proclaimed:

> Rock or a seawall will add weight to the landslide and could reactivate the former landslide along its principle slipping zone.

Komar added that the weight of houses on a "slippery" land mass was not included in the developer's geologic reports and a study of weights against the landform should be undertaken before the city gave final approval for development.

Dave Peden, writing for the *Oregonian* (Feb. 24, 1981) pointed out:

The 9-acre site, owned by former Newport realtor Richard Andersen, now of Portland, has a history of erosion and opponents argue that no matter what steps Andersen takes, someday [his] subdivision will be washed into the Pacific as other homes in the area have done.

On May 5, the *Oregon Journal* editorialized:

Builders should realized ocean is a rough adversary. The Newport Planning Commission has just approved a plan for a site called "Jumpoff Joe." The place is one of the most relentless slide areas on the Oregon coast. Developers propose to control it with a seawall.... Can a seawall defeat the ocean...? The seawall will prove to be inadequate if other seawalls are constructed of rip-rap, large rocks.... Water permeates the rip-rap when waves beat against the jumbled rocks and when a wave retreats, suction removes a little of the earth or sand—a teaspoonful [at a time] perhaps a negligible amount you might think, but the ocean has all the time in the world to collect its teaspoonfuls.

Such measures of protection as seawalls only postpone the confrontation of the sea and the land.

The editorial writer then asks:

Is it fair to future home owners to prepare land, let them build houses costing a quarter of a million dollars then discover that they're really living on a greased slide?

Friends of Lincoln County (FLC), a group formed to oppose the Andersen project known as Beachland Estates, vowed to fight the development. FLC would file an appeal to the Newport City Council, announced FLC President Andrew Goldsmith. He charged, "This is a real attempt by Andersen to unload a parcel of land he feels uncomfortable with. No mention was made that this area is a recent and continuing landslide.

The *News-Times* called the seawall project, "The Great Wall of Newport."

The Nye Beach-Jump Off Joe beach is one of the most well-used on the central coast. A 17-foot [high, 3-foot thick] wall of concrete stretching hundreds of feet is a visual blight

from the beach that will be most difficult to buffer. It most
certainly would be a prime target for graffiti artists.

By mid-summer 1981, the Newport City Council had
asked for legal briefs from the developers of controversial
Beachland Estates and from the Friends of Lincoln County.
A fight was in the works. There was a hassle over filing fees
and a bill for nearly $2,000 for a transcript of an earlier
hearing. Gretchen R. Nelson, of the Friends, observed:

> It is apparent that the City can, and will, use their
> transcript requirements to create an overwhelming obstacle
> for citizens, when they so choose. To be dealt this type of
> adversity by our city govnernment is a disheartening
> experience. Were it not for the rage that has been generated
> by this injustice, the City could have effectively suppressed
> our legal rights by their misguided action.

By January 2, 1982, the City Council had approved the
beachfront development over objections of Friends of
Lincoln County and the Oregon Shores Conservation
Coalition, which had joined to fight city hall. Then an April
21 story in the *Oregonian* announced the Oregon Division of
State Lands denied a permit for the seawall claiming
"Potential adverse impact on public health and safety to the
citizens of the State of Oregon." DSL Director Ed Zajoc
declared:

> I am concerned that the seawall project could produce
> an illusion of safety and security not warranted in a known
> geologic hazard area. The seawall would diminish the
> aesthetic appearance of this section of the beach.

And so the squabble continued.

Andersen had spent more than $250,000 just trying to
get his plans approved and concluded that from a financial
standpoint, the development was no longer feasible. The
developer withdrew his application for a building permit.
But that was not the last to be heard. The Andersens had
defaulted on payments on the property thus the lower
portion immediately south of historic Jump-Off Joe bluff

Ocean Vista Condominiums (top) as seen immediately before project was abandoned after earth slipped, building sagged. Concrete slab (lower) was garage floor seen with large water puddle in center of May 31, 1989 aerial photo by authors.

was sold at auction on December 20, 1982. But this sale did not effect 10 acres at the top of the bluff, a different parcel, on which the Andersens were already at work on 10-unit Ocean Vista condominium.

By spring 1985, framing, walls and roof were all in place. Then the earth "slipped." As Robert J. Ozretich of Newport wrote, "Although the Friends of Lincoln County is being vindicated [in its fight against building on an eroding hillside] the eroding [land] ponderously pulls the condominiums apart...."

After more hearings, the city ordered the building dismantled and the land cleared. All that remains of several years' battles between developers and opponents, and hundreds of thousands of dollars mostly in legal fees, is a slab of concrete at the foot of 11th Street on which a portion of the condo had been placed.

Ozretich concluded:

> Without the [FLC's] tenacity we would now have a crumbled seawall with the rubble of dozens of homes on the beach south of Jump-Off Joe. □

WILLAPA BAY LIGHT

Established October 1, 1858, original building (top, left) lasted until it fell into the sea December 26, 1940. A temporary structure (short tower, center of page) was built nearby. More erosion caused another move to a new, taller tower January 1, 1952 (center, right) but continued damage by erosion caused Coast Guard to move the tower (top, right) again. Due to fear this tower would soon fall, Coast Guard purchased its first modular, "portable," telescoping "upside-down flashlight"-appearing tower (lower, left) which opened June 5, 1986.

CHAPTER 18

WILLAPA BAY
LIGHTHOUSE

In the United States, Willapa Bay lighthouse possibly holds the record for having been moved the greatest number of times, all due to coastal erosion. The operation of the light has always been somewhat of a challenge, first to the United States Lighthouse Service, and later the U.S. Coast Guard. In less than a year, after being established on Cape Shoalwater in 1858, the light shut itself off "automatically" when the keeper ran out of oil for the wick. Isolation was the major problem. No supplies. It was dark for nearly two years. Finally lighted again, the operation continued on this then-isolated point forty miles north of the Columbia River. But the problems changed from no oil, to no land upon which to maintain the lighthouse.

Exactly when the keepers first reported pieces of Cape Shoalwater falling into the sea does not seem to be recorded. But facts are facts. The land was falling away a little at a time at first, then in huge, measured amounts as the years went by.

Erosion became so severe that the Coast Guard built a skeleton steel tower 380 yards east of the building as inspectors were certain the old lighthouse would fall into the sea.

On December 22, 1940, the keeper and crew moved out to safer ground for old King Neptune was undermining the building itself! Jim Gibbs, writing in his book, *Sentinels of the North Pacific*, reported,

> The fickle tides and harbor currents along the north shore of Willapa Harbor from Tokeland to the sea has caused extensive erosion in the last 15 or 20 years [from about 1935]. The erosion cycle causing 1,500 acres of sand to

be swallowed by the sea since 1890...the erosion cutting
away 50 to 100 feet a year.

The 13th Coast Guard District, from its Headquarters
in Seattle, provided a summary of the erosion problems, as
it affected the Coast Guard, in a local *Notice to Mariners.*

> Old structure may be washed out at any time.
> Dec. 22, 1940. Crew abandoned the building.
> Dec. 26, 1940. Old lighthouse has partially collapsed due
> to erosion.
> Dec. 30, 1940. Old lighthouse structure has been carried
> away [and is under more than 50 feet of water].

The winter storm season, established earlier in this
book as being very severe and the highest risk period of the
year, seemed unstoppable at Cape Shoalwater.

The bar channel continually shifts. Depths over the bar
vary from season to season. The Army Corps of Engineers
must continuously inspect and dredge to keep a channel
open for commerce. In *United States Coast Pilot No. 7,* the
U.S. Department of Commerce inserted these lines:

> Buoys marking the channel are moved...because of
> shifting sands and changing channel. Dredging range lights
> are...at the entrance...but they do not necessarily mark
> [safe] water. Vessels should always employ a local pilot due
> to changeable character of the harbor entrance.

Twelve years after the loss of the lighthouse, the Coast
Guard published another *Notice to Mariners.*

> Jan. 1, 1952. Old lighthouse long vanished into the deep
> and ocean is on the rampage now threatening tower that
> replaced original lighthouse. On this date moved to tempo-
> rary wood structure 14 yards northeast of charted position.
> Feb. 15, 1952. Light moved this date to new location [on
> new skeleton steel tower] and light elevation increased to 148
> feet above sea level.
> Dec. 18, 1958 [about 7 years later] Temporarily moved
> to a new location about 15 yards northwest of charted
> position.
> Mar. 12, 1959. Moved to permanent location about
> 1,100 yards northwest from former charted position.

CAPE SHOALWATER, WASHINGTON

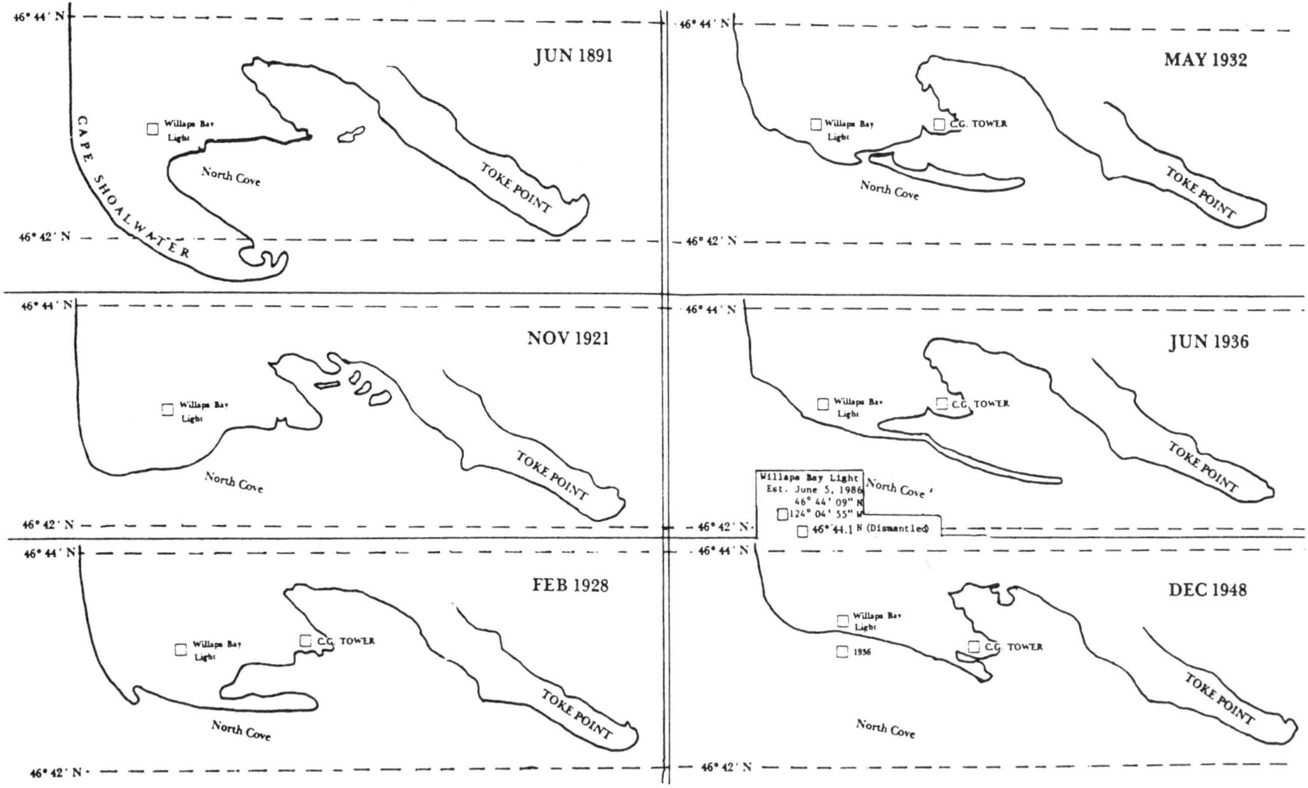

JUN 1891

NOV 1921

FEB 1928

MAY 1932

JUN 1936

DEC 1948

TOKE POINT

North Cove

Willapa Bay Light

C.G. TOWER

CAPE SHOALWATER

Willapa Bay Light
Est. June 5, 1906
46° 44' 09" N
124° 04' 55" W
46° 44.1 N (Dismantled)

1956

46° 44' N

46° 42' N

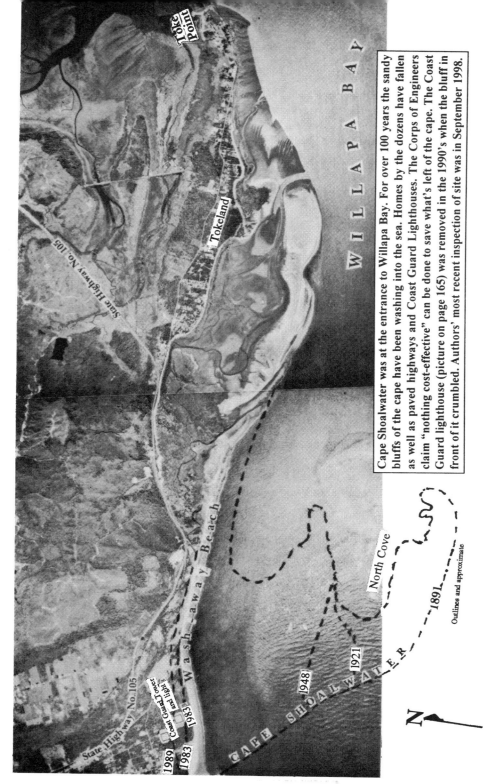

Cape Shoalwater was at the entrance to Willapa Bay. For over 100 years the sandy bluffs of the cape have been washing into the sea. Homes by the dozens have fallen as well as paved highways and Coast Guard Lighthouses. The Corps of Engineers claim "nothing cost-effective" can be done to save what's left of the cape. The Coast Guard lighthouse (picture on page 165) was removed in the 1990's when the bluff in front of it crumbled. Authors' most recent inspection of site was in September 1998.

WILLAPA BAY

Toke Point

Tokeland

State Highway No. 105

Washaway Beach

North Cove

State Highway No. 105

Coast Guard Tower and light

1989 1983 1983

CAPE SHOALWATER

1948

1921

1891

Outlines and approximate

N

The Coast Guard was playing "hop-scotch" with its lighthouse to keep it from falling into the sea. And the concern continues to the present time.

In early 1983, an inspection was carried out by an engineer from the Coast Guard base at Westport. The results were not encouraging.

Back in 1891 when the government bought the present land—1,480 acres—it was considered enough to station a lighthouse as well as to provide for a game preserve. As we have seen, Willapa Light has been moved several times around the property to keep out of erosion's way. The engineer told the authors:

> We have lost 100 yards of ground in the last 20 months. We have 140 yards to go. The light is at the edge of the game reserve and we can't presume to move the light onto that area. At the current rate of erosion, we fear the present position of the light will be undermined in about one year [from January 1983].

He predicted all of the original acreage would be "gone by 1985. We're going to have to do something pretty quick." As we have seen, the Coast Guard was forced to dismantle their tower with light and radio apparatus and install the new modular unit further from the beach.

The Coast Guard was not the only land owner in the "wash-away beach" area to lose acreage and buildings. Scores of summer as well as permanent residences, barns, out-buildings, have been moved or lost over the years. In addition, a section of Highway No. 105 crashed over the edge. On at least one occasion, folks sat in lawn chairs and watched a house fall onto the beach below!

During the year January 1980, January 1981, the Washington Department of Fisheries measured 201 feet washed away with destruction to clam beds. During the 9.9-foot tide on November 21, 1980, the loss was measured at 13½ feet in four hours! Forty-mile winds from the southwest undermined the dune and the dune caved in. When the wind direction swung to the northwest, erosion stopped abruptly. Between April and October, measure-

"Wash-away beach." The post office at North Cove (top) operated from spring 1878 until its business was transferred to Tokeland a short time before the building fell into the sea in 1963. Ellison house (center) toppled in the fall of 1980 as neighbors watched. A section of Highway No 105 (lower) as seen April 30, 1989.

ments indicated there was no loss. But on November 13, neighbors watched sand disappear from the bluff in two days! As the dune disappears, old tree limbs are exposed. Researchers have determined these to be between 100 and 200 years old.

The Washington Department of Fisheries has a keen interest in the area because of shellfish. A spokesman reported that the clam population was decreased due to erosion as well as an intensified interest in public clam digging. In the nine-year period between 1972 and 1981, the clam population decreased from about 2 clams per square yard to 1¼, then ¾ and continues to deplete.

The Fisheries folks have a series of steel posts at 20-foot intervals with which they measure erosion. From January 22, 1980 to December 11, 1981, ten stakes had fallen, or were salvaged at the last moment. The measured loss was just over 300 feet.

Economic losses include loss of cranberry bogs and marketable timber.

In the fall of 1980, excitement gripped people as they watched the ocean chew up a county road, then aim for the Ellison house. Everyone expected the house to fall to the beach below and they were not long waiting. The *Aberdeen Daily World* ran pictures on page 1 on November 14, then again gave the now-lost Ellison house front page coverage two days later.

A little over one year later, the *Daily World* gave front page space to the McGroarty home which was shown perched on the cliff with its back quarters hanging in mid-air. Soon after the owners moved out, the property was vandalized; then on Christmas Day, 1982, it was destroyed by an arsonist. McGroarty recalled he bought four acres and the house about four years earlier. It's all gone!

What has been done to try to stop the devastation?

Local people located about 300 old automobile bodies and engine blocks which they dumped along the eroded shore. The county spent about $15,000 to haul, then dump rocks with the car bodies. Winter storms tore it all apart. (Visitors walk the beach today at low tide and wonder why

Willapa Bay

In an effort to stop erosion at "Wash-away beach," a riprap project included placing fifty automobile bodies and discarded engine blocks along 800-feet of shore. These wrecks were covered with rock. All this washed out in two years. Photograph made March 26, 1973.

engine blocks protrude from the sand!)

The Corps of Engineers was quoted in the Aberdeen newspaper as saying, "Nothing cost effective can be done to save the property."

The highway was relocated in the 1970s and is again about to go. The State watches the road but in 1989 has no funds to move it as a precautionary measure.

A resident announced, "I'll enjoy my home here as long as it lasts, but on stormy winter nights, I don't get much sleep for fear of the sea." □

☆　　　　☆　　　　☆

A Man Who Is Not Afraid Of The Sea Will Soon Be Drowned...

—John Millington Synge [1871-1909]

173

OTHER EROSION AREAS

While the authors have reported on some areas where major erosion has occurred along the Northwest Coast, there are other areas on this coast where the problems have not been as great or as widely known. Some incidents may have had limited local media attention or no mention at all. We include some of these incidents in this Appendix.

The Inn at Spanish Head—Lincoln City

In Lincoln City there is a large hotel, The Inn At Spanish Head. It's a massive concrete and steel structure settled back against a high cliff but with its first floor just few feet above the beach. Architects feel the size and shape of the building

will never permit it to be knocked down by the ocean. But think twice before renting a ground-floor room during a winter storm! Newspaper accounts with pictures illustrate that the sea thinks poorly of this giant. At times the management declines to rent these lower rooms for reason: High tide-driven logs have broken windows and landed in rooms. Iron banisters on outside walkways have been ripped out of their concrete supports. During a winter storm, a man and a woman were standing watching the waves when suddenly a breaker grabbed the woman. The gentleman went home alone!

Ground floor of the Sea Gypsy Motel took water and logs during severe winter storm. Later, motel owners contracted for retaining wall at property's corner where the D River meets the beach.

Sea Gypsy—Lincoln City

In the early 1970s, winter storms wreaked havoc all along the coast. At Lincoln City, an incoming tide piled telephone pole size drift logs in the middle of the U.S. Highway 101 bridge that crosses the D River. In fact, a few logs were found in the river east of the bridge! The Sea Gypsy Motel at the beach, on the north shore at outlet of the river, suffered broken windows along most of its ground floor. When the storms let up, management contracted for a steel-reinforced barricade at the property's corner where that corner meets the beach and the river.

Elk River Spit—Curry County

Writing from Oregon State University Sea Grant College Program on July 28, 1980, Dan Himsworth reported to the authors:

I was at the mouth of the Elk River in Curry County [Oregon] in November of 1977. The river was entering the ocean near Cape Blanco the day before but on this day, waves had breached the 2-mile spit and the entrance was now a mile south of the cape. The next day continued breaching caused the river entrance to move another mile south.

This breaching did not attract the attention of the spit-breaching buffs [or the media].

Cape Lookout State Park

Ever since this park opened in the early 1950s, usage has been high with beachcombers and picnickers as well as over-nighters and week-long vacationers. Of the dozens of state parks along the Oregon coast, Cape Lookout is one of only half-a-dozen that stays open all winter. The beachcombing is best in winter when high seas toss all forms of exciting "junque" onto the shore, especially Japanese glass fishing floats. These severe storms, with accompanying high tides and sharp winds, did not, for the most part, concern winter campers because of the protection afforded them by

Cape Lookout State Park. **(A) Site of beach-access path that had been dug through sand dune probably in 1952. (B) Site of heavy wood bulkhead destroyed by winter storms. (C) 8 campsites, earlier protected from winter winds by dunes, some as high as 50-feet, and trees, now on ledge face open sea too dangerous to use in winter because of washover risk.**

View to seaward from campsites once secluded behind giant dune, now face the sea. The dune was obliterated by coastal erosion.

a dune. This mighty dune was from 30 to 50 feet high and nearly that wide at its base.

A beach access pathway through the dune was dug apparently as part of early park development. Heavy timber bulkheads supported by vertically placed steel girders contained the sand along each side of the path. Lengths of this bulkhead extended at 90 degrees from the mouth of the path to the north and to the south. For many years, decades in fact, this fence kept the seaward side of the dune in place in an effort to protect the dune from the winter season's battering high tides. But at times storm-tossed breakers topped the barricade. As each wave receded, a little of the dune went with it. Over the years the bulkhead timbers rotted.

A series of storms forced breakers through the pathway with sand from the path being carried back to sea each time. Eventually, a channel or "dip" was noticed in the beach extending from the path. From then on, high tides, along with riptides, churned at this weak spot. The breakers battered the bulkhead to oblivion and created an embayment that extends over 200 yards in lenth along the beach.

Sally Webber, member of photographic team that made this picture (June 3, 1989, views remains of once-heavy bulkhead that protected huge dune from the sea.

The original path through the dune, as well as the dune itself, was being obliterated. By winter 1988-89, the great dune had disappeared into the sea. (The sand was redeposited near the entrance to Netarts Bay to the north, engineers say.)

State Park officials, being safety minded, did not permit overnight stays during winter 1988-89 in the sites once protected by the dune as they now face the open ocean. The camps are about 20 feet above the beach. A bath house, once also protected by the dune, is now on the "firing line" for subsequent winter high tides. The propane tank, which provides fuel for the hot showers available in the facility, had to be moved to a new location in early 1989. The former tank site is now part of the beach below. Eight RV sites, with complete hookups, as well as the bath house (and an ampitheatre hidden by trees in our pictures) remain threatened.

What's to be done about this damage to the camp? At this writing State and Federal officials are looking closely at formulas for funding repairs as well as to what method of repair might be the best for the situation. Could this erosion be stopped by using a big piece of cloth? (See Appendix B)

Cabin, which is expected to fall to the beach in winter 1989-90, is about ½ mile north of Raft River, south of Village of Queets, on Washington coast.

Some Other Erosion Areas

Washington's Northwest Coast

For quite a distance along the Washington coast, the public has no access as the land is part of the Quinault Indian Reservation and strictly off-limits to uninvited beachcombers. A colleague, Glenn Barkhurst, who lives in the area and who makes "special purpose" field trips for us, scouted the beach for erosion and found some. In the picture of the boarded up cabin, Barkhurst said the cabin at one time was back from the ledge quite a bit. In spring 1989, following the winter high storm-tides, this cabin's left front corner now is airborne. The building is expected to plunge to the beach, 15-feet below, on a high tide sometime in the winter of 1989-90.

The expected loss of this cabin is by far not the only loss along this beach. Although there are extremely few buildings, devastation to trees growing on top of the ledges, and to the dunes themselves, is pronounced.

Bullards Beach State Park—Bandon

Bullards Beach State Park beach parking area at tip of north jetty on Coquille River at Bandon, was washed over in December 1977, December 1982, again in January 1983. On the 26th the crashing breakers caused the 4-inch thick asphalt lot to buckle and left an assortment of driftwood. Then a mid-March storm sent huge drift logs, some as large as 58 inches in diameter and 10-feet high at the root onto the once popular but now barricaded lot. When the authors viewed the area in March and again in April, it seemed as if the ocean had, indeed, been on a rampage. Should a rip current occur here, would the spit be broken (as at Nestucca) leaving the long abandoned and picturesque lighthouse and north jetty an island? Visitors viewing this scene for the first time will probably not realize this was once a large paved parking lot adjoining one of the better beaches of Southern Oregon—the beach now mostly gone. □

Mid-March 1983 storm tossed huge drift logs (top—photographed by authors on April 4) on parking lot at base of north jetty, Coquille River at Bandon.

Highway 101—Southern Oregon Coast

A few miles north of Gold Beach, near the Ophir Safety Rest Area, a section of Highway No. 101 fell onto the beach from its perch atop a high sand bluff. In this instance one might compare this loss with that at Bayocean when the 140-foot high dune was knocked down over 40 years earlier. Following an extensive and experimental method of repair, the highway was restored. (See Appendix B)

Cannon Beach—North Oregon Coast

On February 19, 1973, the authors watched the high tide strike the sea wall at this building recently converted to apartments, on Cannon Beach. Building has been there for decades and is subject to severe winter battering by tides carrying huge, deadly drift logs.

Winchuck River Estuary

Estuary of Winchuck River. The Winchuck is only half a mile north of the Oregon-California line with low sand dunes on the south of the river's mouth and steep but low headland to the north. During winter storms it is common, in some years, for huge deposits of driftwood to accumulate on both sides of the river and in the small bay to the south. Other years' storms the high tides may totally remove the logs, all of which are extremely unstable to walk on. In the mid-1970s when the river's mouth became dammed by sand build-up, some local men seriously considered bulldozing the entrance, only to discover a new entrance had naturally occurred about 100 yards to the south. In time this second mouth for the river closed and the original channel again opened.

HOLDING BACK THE SEA
WITH A PIECE OF CLOTH

Bert Webber at the site of Highway No. 101 "repair" on the south Oregon coast near Ophir Safety Rest Area. (See photo "Highway 101" page 182.)

We have seen where people who owned houses in the path of crawling erosion had hurriedly contracted with truckers to dump rocks on their frontages in an effort to stop, or at least delay, the approaching sea. We have also seen especially at Siletz (Salishan) Spit, that a stormy sea will roar over these piles of rocks (riprap) as if they had not been placed. We are further reminded that the people around North Cove at Cape Shoalwater placed wrecked car bodies and engine blocks along the shore in an attempt to stop the on-rushing sea—to no avail.

Bayocean

What are scientists doing to find a better way of protecting frontages which are in the path of crashing breakers?

One approach is with fabric. Textiles. Geotextiles.

Geotextiles are permeable, synthetic fabrics which may be incorporated into a structure to stabilize the edge of a sand dune facing the ocean. Likewise, these materials might be used to strengthen riprap placed on a collapsing dune.

While this science is young, substantial research has been underway for some years, both in the United States and overseas.

The Sea Grant College Program at Oregon State University, Corvallis, Oregon, has been very active in research about the sea. William McDougal completed a doctoral dissertation on the subject of "Ocean Wave-Soil-Geotextile Interaction." This is listed in the General References.

It is not always easy to find a source of appropriate size rock close to a beach-protection project, thus geotextiles for coastal and ocean structures appear important. Further, in most areas the dumping of gravel and rock without prearranged permits is no longer possible due to importance of protecting marine environment. In some areas the use of aggregate may not be indicated at all. Geotextile applications in coastal engineering include: erosion protection for piers, buildings, foundation stabilization for sea walls, jetties, etc.

Geotextiles are constructed as woven, non-woven and combination materials. The properties of the geotextile vary with the type fabric and the planned use. Some important performance functions include: drainage, filtration, reinforcement, separation and armor. The fabric must also be of such strength that it will last the expected life of the structure it is to protect. In addition to withstanding the pounding of the sea, the geotextile must have resistance to clogging, tearing, ultraviolet deterioration, puncturing, and other forces.

McDougal and Charles K. Sollitt, writing in *Analytical Modeling of Geotextiles in Ocean Engineering Applications*,

186

point out that "no analytical procedures are presently [1981] available to predict the behavior of a soil-geotextile combination interacting with ocean waves. Specifically, the method does not exist for the [project] engineer to examine the in-place behavior of alternative geotextiles to seek an improved state of stress in a marine foundation."

Probably, now that the experimental repair of Highway No. 101 has been completed, technical studies will be forthcoming.

Is it possible that builders will, some day, include geotextiles in their specifications for houses they plant on sand dunes in the face of a restless sea? □

APPENDIX C

T. B. POTTER'S TRANSPORTATION

Motor Vessel *Bayocean*

Built	1911
Length	150 feet
Beam	18 feet

Bayocean

Propulsion	Single screw
Fuel	Gasoline
Engines	Speedway 150-Hp (2)
	Speedway 175-Hp
	(engines in tandem)
Passengers	Berthed: 50
	Lounge: 50
Crew	Captain, Mate, 6 seamen

Although both Potters had left real estate, it is presumed their former company lost the yacht as part of bankruptcy proceedings. The ship passed time tied up in the Willamette River, but precise data for this period, until late spring 1918, has not been discovered.

Vessel was purchased by the United States Navy in June 1918 within a program to acquire then convert large seagoing private yachts to armed patrol vessels. (A similar project existed also in World War II.)

The ship was commissioned in the Navy as Patrol Boat *Bayocean* (SP-2640) on August 17, 1918. Frequently the Navy discontinued a ship's original name but in this instance the "civilian" name was retained. The Navy used their own measurements in registering the ship:

Displacement	130 tons
Draft	7 feet, 6 inches
Speed	13 knots

To properly equip the yacht for naval service, two 3-inch guns were installed—one fore and one aft.

Crew	19 officers and men

Some interior remodeling was done to provide an officers' wardroom. Available data does not indicate which naval facility made these conversions.

Lieutenant Vinal S. Terry (USN 37445) was ordered aboard as Commanding Officer. Lt. Terry sailed his ship to San Diego, arriving there September 11, 1918. The ship was assigned to the Pacific Fleet, Division No. 2. Duty: Mail carrier and patrol *Bayocean* did this just for a short time— only until November 20. The First World War was over by this time so why a ship was sent on a mission to patrol of

Pichilinque, Mexico,—foreign service—is undetermined. Nevertheless, that was the order. This sea duty lasted six days then the ship went back to San Diego.

On February 3, 1919, we find the vessel in dock at Mare Island Navy Yard, Vallejo, California. One naval historian wise-cracked, "She was probably so wobbly in the sea nobody could keep their stomach settled long enough to stand muster let alone tend to duty!"

Apparently *Bayocean* stayed in dock until decommissioning ceremonies on March 14, 1919.

Exactly where the yacht waited for her next adventure has not been found, but she was sold by the Navy on August 5, 1921. Her history becomes clouded after being dropped from the Navy List of Ships. One source claims she was owned by Crowley Launch and Tug Company of San Francisco. Possible? The yacht had been designed as a passenger ship and there was good sight-seeing business on San Francisco Bay. But correspondence with that firm's successor, Crowley Maritime Corporation, in spring 1981, stated the firm's senior person "has no recollection of the company owning such a vessel."

What happened to *Bayocean*? Standard reference sources do not record the ship further. Could this once fine yacht still be "seasicking" its riders in some foreign port?

The authors are aware of a ship *Bayocean* listed in the American Bureau of Shipping lists for 1923. Here a ship of this name appears, owned by Bay Ocean (2 words) Excursion Company of San Francisco. Listings in the 1925 through 1928 lists show the owner as W. J. Sturpanant, still with a San Francisco registry. But there is a difference. Data for this "second" *Bayocean* lists 150 tons and deck length of 130.1 feet. If this is the same whip, she's grown 20 tons heavier and 20 feet shorter (not polite for a "lady" in her old age)!

Potter's Railroad Car

Direct descendants have no first-hand knowledge of their grandfather's use or exploits of the railroad car. But

Private Car *Louisiana*

two of the three recalled hearing remarks that he indeed had
such a car. John Potter Dobbins produced, from family
archives, the manufacturer's specifications and remarked,
"He [Potter] had a private car that came from the
Exposition in St. Louis."

This car was built specifically for exhibiting at the
Louisiana Purchase Exposition, 1904, on a Pullman basic
specification by the Hicks Locomotive & Car Works. The
authors determined, by comparing these specifications with
the data from ten special cars built for the fair, from sheets
furnished by the St. Louis Art Museum, that the spec sheet
owned by Dr. Dobbins matched the description for one of
only two "observation" cars built for the fair. Recalling
that the base blue print was Pullman, ("Ground Plan No.
1000, over platforms coupled, 75'0'',") we looked to
identify special appointments. Dobbins' sheet indicates the
"Private Room" was "vermilion" wood. The specifications from the Art Museum were very clear that each car
had different interior appointments. Only one, *Louisiana*,
had vermilion, a rare redwood from the Andaman Islands.

It is not established whether Potter bought the car or leased it at the close of the fair. Recalling that T. B. Potter withdrew from real estate about 1910 when he became ill, one could presume the car, if owned, was sold, or if leased, was turned back at that time. There seems no mention of the car during the tenure of his son, T. Irving Potter, as head of the firm. □

APPENDIX D

POTTER'S MARK

It has been said that an architect leaves his mark on history by the buildings he designed that stand long after he's gone—unless the building is torn down.

A real estate developer's name seems assured in history if the site he developed is platted, people move in, and it isn't subdivided by somebody else.

It seems doubtful that Thomas Benton Potter had any plans to perpetuate his name in this manner as none of his several developments carry his name. Nevertheless, Potter left his mark in the records as well as in the name of his daughter, Arleta, on places.

Potter's developments, and sales opportunities on developments of others, appear to have been between 1902 and 1907. He covered a lot of ground in a very short time.

In Kansas City, Missouri, T. B. Potter was the promoter and salesman for the Marlborough Heights Addition. This section, then on the southern outskirts of the city, ran for about one mile along 71st, 72nd and 73rd Streets to the Jackson County line. A little later he acquired ownership but he does not appear to have maintained any residence in Missouri. The *R. L. Polk Kansas City Directory* has no listing for Potter in any editions prior to 1907 (by which time he was well-entrenched in his Bayocean Project). In the 1907 directory we find a large bold-face type advertisement under "POTTER T B REALTY CO" identifying "(T B Potter) owner Marlborough Heights 416 R A Long bldg both tels Main 4150."

Three lines down (page No. 1135) for his personal listing, we find:

> Potter, Thos B (T B Potter Realty Co
> 416 R A Long bldg) r San Francisco Cal

The little "r" gives location of his "residence."

A letterhead from family archives indicates he moved from the Long Building to the Waldheim Building, but no further entry was found in the city directory.

At the same time, according to the letterhead, he also had offices in San Jose, Half Moon Bay and in San Francisco, California, as well as in Portland, Oregon. His office in San Francisco was Room 901 Monadnock Building, 681 Market Street. The building is adjacent to the Financial District.

The Assessor for San Mateo County, California (about 15 miles south of San Francisco), determined in 1989 that T. B. Potter platted a subdivision on the outskirts of the City

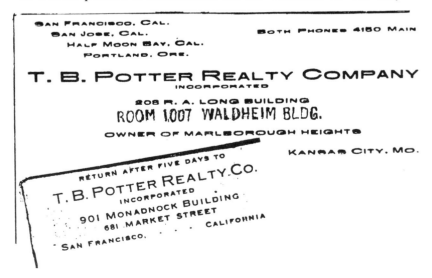

of Half Moon Bay in early September, 1906. The County Board of Supervisors accepted it as Arleta Park on September 17. The area is along Ocean Boulevard and thrives to the present time.

In the meantime, Potter was engaged also in real estate development east of Portland. His major activity there appears to have been between 1902-04. He again honored his daughter by naming the community Arleta. As people moved in, the Mt. Scott trolley line placed a station at what is now Foster Road and S.E. 65th Street. The traction company named the stop Arleta Station.

Due to the growing number of children in the area, Multnomah County School District No. 47 started a school and called it Arleta School. Although the building has been replaced at least twice, today's Arleta School is at 5109 S.E. 66th St. and is now a part of Portland School District No. 1-J.

With so many people coming in, a better way was needed to handle mail.

Following a petition drive, the United States Post Office Department opened an office in the vicinity of Foster Road and Holgate Street. The post office was officially entered as Arleta, Oregon.

193

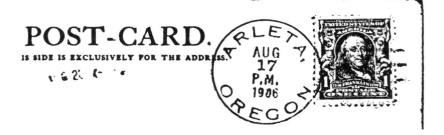

POST-CARD.
IS SIDE IS EXCLUSIVELY FOR THE ADDRESS.

ARLETA
AUG
17
P.M.
1906
OREGON

About 1904, some folks formed a new church. The outgrowth was Arleta (American) Baptist Church. Today's building is at 4515 S.E. 64th Street.

The name, Arleta, did not find its way into Potter's Bayocean Park. This may be because the teenaged Arleta Potter did not like it, being too young to appreciate the honor her proud father had bestowed on her. As she grew older, she became so displeased with the use of her name, when she reached the age of majority, she went to court and legally changed it to Natalia. (Natalia Potter attended the University of California, then married John L. Dobbins. The couple went to China where her husband was Dean at the College of Engineering at Peking. Her two sons, David and John, were born in China. She died in Santa Barbara in 1973.)

T. B. Potter retired from real estate development when in his forties due to illness. As we have seen, his son, T. Irving Potter took the helm. We also saw that his son discovered the spit upon which Bayocean Park was developed. When his father departed about 1910, the son continued the business.

Both Potter's had left the T. B. Potter Realty Company by about 1915. The son, who was an inventor of intricate mechanical things, followed this line in its various forms for the rest of his life. His father, who had bought the mansion in Alameda in 1912, lived there as well as on Mason Street in what would today be called downtown San Francisco.

Of the various Potter adventures in real estate development, the only one that met disaster was Bayocean. The

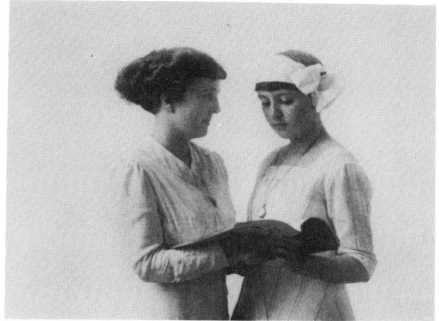

Mary Frances (Mrs. T. B.) Potter and daughter Arleta when the girl was a young teenager. The girl became so upset that her father's real estate developments had her name, she legally changed it to Natalia.

coastal erosion that tore the spit apart was not Potter's fault. The story and history of the development on the spit springs up in many aspects of Oregon history, coastal geology and oceanography. Potter's name will always remain a vital part of the history of real estate development in Oregon even though the site of his famous "Atlantic City of the West" is today vacant acreage. □

| 1909 | PORTLAND CITY DIRECTORY | 407 |

BAYOCEAN WILL BE KNOWN AS THE BEACH RESORT OF THE NORTHWEST

| 1909 | PORTLAND CITY DIRECTORY | 423 |

Potter-Chapin Realty Company
No. 514 Corbett Building   Owner BAYOCEAN

ABOUT THE AUTHORS

Bert and Margie Webber have collaborated on several books about what they call "the fantastic Pacific Northwest." In addition to the present work, they co-authored *Maimed By the Sea*, an earlier documentary on coastal erosion, as well as *Beachcombing and Camping Along the Northwest Coast*; *Jacksonville, Oregon, The Making of a National Historic Landmark*; *Oregon's Great Train Holdup Bandits Murder 4—Didn't Get a Dime!*, and *Railroading in Southern Oregon*. In addition, Bert has done many other books, including major revisions. He also writes introductions, provides photographs to enhance the works of others and designs books and dust jackets.

Bert Webber is a research photojournalist. In World War II, among various assignments, he was a Signal Corps cameraman and photolab technician in Alaska and in Europe. Later, he graduated in Journalism from Whitworth College, did graduate work at Portland State University assisted by a grant from the Oregon Association of School Librarians, then earned his Master of Library Science Degree at the University of Portland on a Tangley Oakes Graduate Fellowship. He has written articles since his teen years which have been published nationally, regionally and locally. Many are listed in the *Reader's Guide to Periodical Literature*. For five years he was a school librarian and also taught Northwest History. He is frequently seen and heard on TV and radio talkshows (including NBC TODAY and WGN-radio late-night talkshow guest) on subjects from his books. Bert Webber is listed in *Who's Who in the West* and in *Contemporary Authors*.

Margie Webber is a recently retired Registered Professional Nurse. She earned her baccalaureate degree in Nursing from the University of Washington by first working in the photo-finishing darkrooms for the Bartell Drug Company in Seattle. Then, with a scholarship from Kellogg Foundation, she trained as a member of the United States Cadet Nurse Corps during World War II. She worked in a variety of positions and did graduate work at University of Washington, Portland State University and at Oregon State University. She contributed to nursing papers. For the present work she is copy and picture editor. Margie also takes active part in field trips to all the erosion-prone areas in this book. She is an acute observer of beach conditions and she is constantly on the lookout for agates and for those elusive Japanese glass fishing floats.

The Webbers, who have always been "possibility thinkers," enjoy working with people, love to travel and do so regularly for their books. They make their home in Oregon's Rogue River Valley. They have four children and several grandchildren. □

GENERAL REFERENCES

Books

Armstrong, Chester H. *Oregon State Parks History 1917-1963*. Oregon State Highway Div., 1965.

Bennitt, Mark (Ed.) *History of the Louisiana Purchase Exposition.* Universal Exposition Publishing Co. (St. Louis) 1905.

Culp, Edwin D. *Stations West; The Story of Oregon Railways.* Caxton, 1972.

Gibbs, James [Jim] A. *Oregon's Seacoast Lighthouses.* Webb Research Group, 1992.

_____. *Sentinels of the North Pacific.* Binford & Mort, 1955.

McHarg, Ian L. *Design With Nature.* Natural History Press, 1969.

Orcutt, Ada M. *Tillamook, Land of Many Waters.* Binford & Mort, 1951.

Shepard, Francis P. and Harold R. Wanless. *Our Changing Coastline.* McGraw, 1972.

Steele, E. N. *The Immigrant Oyster (Ostrea Gigas).* Pacific Coast Oyster Growers Assn., 1964.

Webber, Bert. *What Happened at Bayocean—Is Salishan Next?* Ye Galleon Press, 1978.

Webber, Bert and Margie. *Beachcombing and Camping Along the Northwest Coast.* Ye Galleon Press, 1978.

_____. *Maimed By the Sea.* Ye Galleon Press, 1983.

Government Documents

House Doc. No. 217   55th Cong.   2nd Session   Jan. 11, 1898

House Doc. No. 965   60th Cong.   1st Session   May 22, 1908

House Doc. No. 349   62nd Cong.   2nd Session   Dec. 21, 1911

Public Law No. 685   75th Cong.   Chapter 535-3rd Session   Jun. 20, 1938

House Doc. No. 650   80th Cong.   2nd Session   May 3, 1948

Senate Doc. No. 8   83rd Cong.   2nd Session   apr. 1, 1954

United States Coast Pilot; Pacific Coast. 18th Ed. U.S. Department of Commerce, 1982.

Light List; Pacific Coast, United States. U.S. Department of Commerce, Lighthouse Service, 1934.

Light List; Pacific Coast and Pacific Islands. Vol. III. Department of Transportation, U.S. Coast Guard, 1983.

General References

Special Studies

Baliga, B. R. and Robert Hudspeth. *Evaluation of Sand Waves In an Estuary.* (ORESU-R-81-003) Sea Grant College Program, Oregon State Univ., 1981.

Beach Patrol History. Compiled by War Diary Office, 13th U.S. Naval Dist., Seattle, n.d.

Breese, Wilbur P. and William Q. Wick. *Oyster Farming.* Marine Advisory Program Sea Grant Bulletin No. 13. Oregon State Univ., 1981.

Byrne, John V. and William B. North. *Landslides of Oregon: North Coast.* Dept. of Oceanography, Oregon State Univ., 1971.

———— and Daniel A. Panshin. *Continental Sediments Off Oregon.* Marine Advisory Program Sea Grant Bulletin No. 8, Oregon State Univ., 1972.

Dicken, Samuel N. *Final Report: Some Recent Physical Changes on the Oregon Coast.* Office of Naval Research, Geography Dept., Univ. of Oregon, 1961.

Environmental Resource Analysis: Neskowin to Tillamook, Oregon. Oregon State Highway Div., June 1970.

An Inventory of Filled Land in Tillamook Bay Estuary. Adv. Comm. to the State Land Board, Salem, Aug. 1972.

Katz, Barbara and Stephen R. Gabriel. *Oregon's Ever-changing Coastline [Learning About the Ocean].* Extension Marine Advisory Program SG-35 Land Grant/Sea Grant Cooperative Program. Oregon State Univ., 1977.

Komar, Paul D. *Beach Sand Transport: Distribution and Total Drift.* (ORESU-R-77-007) Sea Grant Program, Oregon State Univ., 1977.

————. *Wave Conditions on the Oregon Coast During the Winter of 1977-78 and the Resulting Erosion of Nestucca Spit.* (ORESU-R-78-014) Sea Grant Program, Oregon State Univ., 1978.

———— and Barbara Ann McKinney. *The Spring 1976 Erosion of Siletz Spit, Oregon; With an Analysis of the Causative Wave and Tide Conditions.* (ORESU-T-77-004) Sea Grant Program, Oregon State Univ., 1977.

———— and Thomas A. Terich. *Changes Due to Jetties at Tillamook Bay, Oregon.* (ORESU-R-77-016) Sea Grant Program, Oregon State Univ., 1977.

———— and Wm. Quinn, Clayton Creech, C. Cary Rea, Jose R. Lizarrage-Arciniega. *Wave Conditions and Beach Erosion on the Oregon Coast.* (ORESU-R-76-010) Sea Grant Program, Oregon State Univ., 1976.

McDougal, William G. *et al. Ocean Wave-Soil-Geotextile Interaction.* (ORESU-X-82-001) Sea Grant Program, Oregon State Univ., 1982.

Bayocean

and Charles K. Sollitt. *Analytical Modeling of Geotextiles in Ocean Engineering.* [Abstract] Ocean Engineering Program, Dept. Civil Engr., Oregon State Univ., 1981.

Murray, Thomas J. (& Assoc.) *Report on Port Facilities and Potential at Tillamook Bay, Ore.* Private Print, 1960.

National Shoreline Study: Inventory Report, the Columbia—North Pacific Region, Washington and Oregon. Portland Dist. U.S. Army Corps of Engineers, 1971.

Prestedge, Gordon K. *Stabilization of Landslides Along the Oregon Coast.* (ORESU-X2-77-003) Sea Grant Program, Oregon State Univ., 1977.

Rea, Campbell C. *Erosion of Siletz Spit, Oregon.* (ORESU-X2-74-012) Sea Grant Program, Oregon State Univ., 1974.

Rip Currents, Rhythmic Topography, Edge Waves, and the Erosion of Beaches. (Research/Coastal Environments Project No. R/CP-17) Investigators: Paul D. Komar and Robert A. Holman. NOAA/Sea Grant Program, Oregon State Univ., 1981.

Schlicker, Herbert G. "Environmental Geology of the Coastal Region of Tillamook and Clatsop Counties, Oregon," in *Bulletin No. 74*, State of Oregon Dept. of Geology and Mineral Industries, July 1972.

Tillamook Bay. (Task Force Report) Extension Service Special Rpt. No. 462, Oregon State Univ., Nov., 1976.

Tunon, Nicholas A. A. *Beach Profile Changes and Onshore-Offshore Sand Transport on the Oregon Coast.* (ORESU-X2-7702) Sea Grant Program, Oregon State Univ.

Wick, William Q. *Crisis in Oregon Estuaries.* Marine Advisory Program Sea Grant Bulletin No. 4, Oregon State Univ., 1970.

Periodicals

Lund, Ernest. "Coastal Landforms Between Tillamook Bay and the Columbia River," in *The Ore Bin.* State of Oregon Dept. of Geology and Mineral Industries, Nov. 1972.

"The Last Winter," in *Pacific Northwest Sea.* Oceanographic Commission of Washington, Fall 1971.

Pamphlets

Oregon Salmon Fishing. Travel Information Dept., Oregon State Highway Div., Salem, n.d.

Let's Clam in Tillamook County. Tillamook County Chamber of Commerce, Tillamook, n.d.

Newspapers
(listed chronologically)

"Announce 1911 Bayocean Plans; Big Coast Resort Being Rapidly Made Available for Coming Season's Enjoyment—Hotel Soon to Open," in *Oregon Daily Journal*, Dec. 31, 1910, p. 10.

200

General References

"First Regular Train Service is Run to Coast Town," in Bayocean *Surf*, Dec. 1, 1911, p. 1.

"Miles Completed; All Lots at Bayocean Accessible," in *Surf*, Apr. 1, 1912.

"Assurance of Future Dirt Flying at Bayocean," in *Surf* [Bayocean]. Jan. 1, 1912.

"Thomas Irving Potter in His Variety," in *The Spectator* [Portland, Ore.]. May 18, 1912, p. 10.

"Seas Wreck Newport Fill," in *Oregon Journal*, Feb. 8, 1940, p. 1.

"House Tumbles Into Widening Gap at Newport. . ." in *Oregon Journal*, March 31, 1943, p. 1.

"Earth Wiggles Beach Houses; Newport Residents Forced to Move," in *Oregonian*, Apr. 1, 1943, p. 6.

"Bayocean Town Faces Threat of Being Destroyed," in Tillamook *Headlight-Herald*, Jan. 5, 1949, p. 1.

"Highest Tide and Wind in 30 Years Strike Rockaway; Property Badly Damaged," in Tillamook *Headlight-Herald*, Jan. 5, 1949, p. 1.

"Engineers Believe Rock Dike in Tillamook Bay Might Save Sea-Battered Bayocean Peninsula," in *Oregonian*, Jan. 8, 1953, p. 4.

"Huge Storms Smash Bayocean Survival Hopes," in *Oregonian*, Jan. 18, 1953, p. 24.

"Salishan Spit Residents Sue," in *News Guard*, Dec. 27, 1973.

"Vicious Storm Hammers Oregon Coast; 3 Persons Hurt, Damage High," in *Oregonian*, Feb. 19, 1976, p. 1.

"Siletz Battle With Sea Intensifies," in *Oregon Journal*, Mar. 14, 1977, p. 1.

"Bayocean Breached 25 Years Ago Sunday," in Tillamook *Headlight-Herald*, Nov. 16, 1977, p. 6.

"Jump-Off Joe Quagmire Is A Travesty," in Newport *News-Times*, Feb. 4, 1981.

"Jump-Off Joe Development Criticized," in Newport *News-Times*, Feb. 18, 1981.

"Geologist Claims Jump-Off Joe Site Work Will Enhance Stability," in Newport *News-Times*, Feb. 18, 1981, p. 2.

"OSU Geologist Attacks Jump-Off Joe Report," in *Sunday Oregonian*, Mar. 24, 1981.

"Builders Should Realize Ocean is a Rough Adversary," in *Oregon Journal*, May 5, 1981, p. 14.

"FLC [Friends of Lincoln County] Vows to Fight Development," in *The Lincoln Log* [Newport, Ore.], May 26, 1981, p. 1.

"Jump-Off Joe Woes," in *News-Times*, May 27, 1981.

"Development Opponents Protest $1,930 Fee for Hrg [Hearing] Transcript," in *News-Times*, Jun. 24, 1981.

"Transcript Fee Out Of Line," in *News-Times*, n.d. [1981].

"Legal Battle Continues Over Jump-Off Joe Subdivision Try," in *News-Times*, Jul. 8, 1981.

"State Denies Jumpoff Joe Seawall Permit, Developers Request Hearing," in *Oregonian*, Apr. 21, 1982.

"Jumpoff Joe Plans Changes—Owners Want Condominiums," in *News-Times*, Feb. 23, 1982.

"Jumpoff Joe Land Sold After Payment Default," in *News-Times*, Dec. 28, 1982.

"Application Withdrawn For Wall Permit," in *News-Times*, Mar. 9, 1983.

"Dreams For Land Sunk Slowly Into Sea," in *Oregonian*, Jun. 1, 1985.

Unpublished Manuscript

Dalquist, Ellen, *Bayocean, the Ghost City of Dreams.*

ILLUSTRATION CREDITS

Illustrations not credited are by the authors.
(AC) author collection.

frontis. Burford Wilkerson
vi Greta Forbish
14 John Potter Dobbins col.
16, 17 (AC)
19, 20 (AC)
21 John Potter Dobbins col.
23, 24 (AC)
29 (AC)
31 (AC)
33 Burford Wilkerson (top)
34, 35 (AC)
37, 38 (AC)
40 (AC)
41 John Potter Dobbins col.
42 Tillamook County Assessor
44 John Potter Dobbins col.
45, 46 (AC)
47 Mrs. Russell Hoover (top)
48 (AC)
54 Mrs. Russell Hoover col.
56 Howard A. Mader (top, left); others (AC)
57 (AC)
59 Howard Sherwood
61, 62 Erma Lewis
63 (AC)
64 Dale B. Webber
67 Jean R. Hopkins

68 (AC)
70 Dale B. Webber (right)
76 (AC)
77 Howard Sherwood
78 (AC)
80 Howard Sherwood
81 (AC)
82 Greta Forbish
84 Jean R. Hopkins (top); Corps of Engrs (lower)
85 Howard Sherwood
86 (AC)
88 Greta Forbish (top); (AC lower)
90-91, 93-94 Greta Forbish
95 Mrs. Russell Hoover col.
96 (AC)
98, 99, 101-103 Greta Forbish
104 Howard Sherwood
105 Greta Forbish
107 (AC)
108 Corps of Engrs
110 (AC)
111 (AC top)
112 Delores Snyder
118 Dale B. Webber
122 Dale B. Webber (top, left); Sally Webber (top, right)

123 Corps of Engrs
126 U.S. Geological Survey
128 Geoffery Madden (top)
132 (AC)
133 Corps of Engrs
138 (AC)
149 Sea Grant Program (map)
150, 151 State of Oregon Dept of Transportation
157 Lincoln County Hist. Soc.
159 Yaquina Art Assn (top, center)
163 Newport *News-Times* (top)
165 (AC, top, lower, right); Don McArthur (top, right)
168 Don Johnson, USCG
169 Corps of Engrs
171 (AC top & center)
174 (AC)
178, 179 Dale B. Webber
180 Glenn Barkhurst
187 (AC)
190 (AC)
192 (AC)
193 Dale B. Webber
194 Richard W. Helbock col.
195 John Potter Dobbins col. (top); (AC, lower)

INDEX

Index

Index

Index